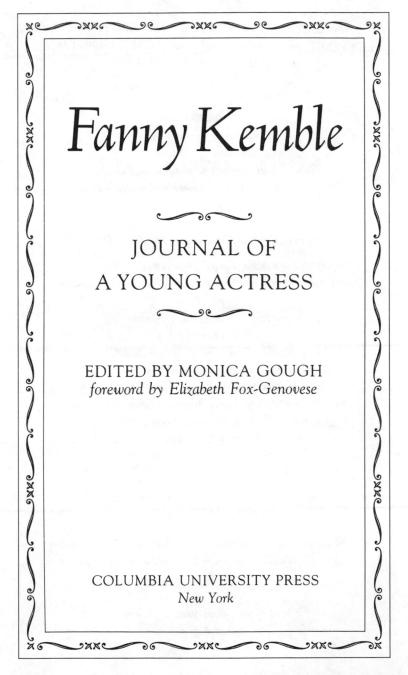

Fanny Kemble

JOURNAL OF A YOUNG ACTRESS

EDITED BY MONICA GOUGH
foreword by Elizabeth Fox-Genovese

COLUMBIA UNIVERSITY PRESS
New York

Frontispiece: MISS FANNY KEMBLE after SIR THOMAS
LAWRENCE, an engraving on steel by C. PICART, published 1831
(collection Manchester City Art Galleries).

Columbia University Press
New York   Oxford
Preface, notes copyright © 1990 Monica Gough
Foreword copyright © 1990 Columbia University Press
All rights reserved

Library of Congress Cataloging-in-Publication Data

Kemble, Fanny, 1809–1893.
Fanny Kemble: journal of a young actress/edited by Monica Gough.
p. cm.
Includes bibliographical references.
ISBN 0-231-07036-5
1. Kemble, Fanny, 1809–1893—Diaries.
2. Kemble, Fanny, 1809–1893—Journeys—United States.
3. United States—Description and travel—1783–1848.
4. Actors—Great Britain—Diaries.
I. Gough, Monica. II. Title. III. Title: Journal of a young actress.
PN2598.K4A3 1990
792'.028'092–dc20
[B]
89–38628
CIP

Casebound editions of Columbia University Press books are Smyth-
sewn and printed on permanent and durable acid-free paper
∞
Book design by Jennifer Dossin

Printed in the United States of America
c 10 9 8 7 6 5 4 3 2 1

For Hugh

CONTENTS

FOREWORD

Proud, high-spirited, and, withal, not entirely unselfcritical, Frances Anne Kemble embarked on August 1, 1832, with her father, Charles Kemble, the actor, for an acting tour of the United States in the hopes of restoring the family's fortunes. Kemble, always known as Fanny, had launched her career as an actress three years previously when she had made her debut as Juliet at Covent Garden with a similar object. Her success launched her career and temporarily helped her father, but did not solve the long term problems. The American tour, which lasted from September 1832 to June 1834, brought the desired professional and financial success and, at its conclusion, Kemble's marriage to Pierce Butler, the heir to a great slaveholding fortune, who had assiduously courted her during her appearance in Philadelphia.

Throughout the tour Kemble kept a journal that she published in 1835 over the intransigent objections of her husband. The initial impetus for publication came from Kemble's determination to earn some money to provide for her beloved aunt, Dall (her mother's sister, Adelaide De Camp), who had accompanied her on the tour and been injured when a carriage overturned. Dall died as a result of those injuries, and the pressing need for money dissipated. Yet Kemble persisted in her plans for publication. Even after her husband deleted all proper names, knowledgeable contemporaries could, with little difficulty, recognize many of the people who figure in her pages. Pierce Butler strenuously objected to Kemble's frank and unflattering depiction of Americans and America. Undoubtedly, he objected to his wife's publishing at all. For as Mrs. Pierce Butler, Fanny Kemble had joined a world in which respectable married ladies did not normally write for publication.

Today, Frances Anne Kemble is best known as a writer for her celebrated *Journal of a Residence on a Georgian Plantation, 1838–39*, written during a brief stay on Pierce Butler's Sea Island plantations. That journal, published in 1863, constituted a deliberate intervention in the war against slavery, and perhaps a personal attack on the husband from whom she had acrimoniously parted. As a direct, personal testimony to the iniquities of slavery, and as a detailed account of everyday life on a slave plantation, it has ranked among the most widely influential accounts of the antebellum South.

Any close reader of the *Journal of a Residence*, especially one who also knows something of that Southern slave society which Kemble was indicting, cannot but recognize the extent to which she crafted her narrative for maximum polemical effect. Under the veneer of a straightforward account of ordinary life amidst slaveholders and slaves, she dramatically rendered scenes and encounters designed to represent the aspects of the system that most appalled her— notably, the unchecked power of the master, the assault on the spirit as well as the bodies of the slaves. Kemble unmistakably intended to juxtapose the hierarchy and dependence of slave society with the upstanding individualism and personal independence of free (bourgeois) society. From this contrast, Kemble herself emerges as the unswerving defender of the values of work, initiative, and individual responsibility.

Like the *Journal of a Residence*, this journal of Kemble's first visit to the United States, her twenty-two-month tour as an actress, properly belongs to the genre of travelers' accounts. But also like the *Journal of a Residence*, it must be recognized as something more. For, in depicting American society, Kemble was, however covertly, self-consciously depicting herself.

An accomplished actress and a skillful and graceful writer, not to mention a highly self-aware and politically astute woman, Kemble must be credited with multiple purposes in writing and publishing her journals. Not least, she must be credited with scrupulous attention to the representation of herself offered to public scrutiny. The problem of Kemble's self-representation commands particular attention because, by normal criteria, her journals did not focus—or focused only peripherally—on self-representation. Given the genteel and cultivated surface of travel narrative, the present journal in particular challenges us to mobilize all the strategies of reading that literary critics have been developing.

Stylistically, Kemble relies upon informality and apparent spontaneity to establish the tone and structure of her narrative. Embarking on an adventure, exploring a new world, she is simply keeping a record of people and places, manners and morals. She writes as if writing for herself alone. This strategy permits her, without apparent inconsistency, to write only of those objects, customs, and events, that capture her attention. Although the pretense of providing a full chronicle provides the principal structure of the narrative, it remains a pretense—a useful stylistic convenience that relieves her of the obligation to impose a more artful narrative structure.

Throughout the journal a cluster of key events recurs frequently enough to afford the reader a sense of her daily life: meals, horseback rides, social gatherings, appearances at the theater. Beyond these, she most commonly writes of trips, outings, social events, or noteworthy people. Intermittently, she offers descriptions of particular places or scenery. And always she interpolates personal comments on weather, food, dress, behavior, literature. Occasionally, she offers arresting observations on the American scene, but, overall, she fails to provide the acute commentaries and telling judgments for which we still read Frances Trollope, Harriet Martineau, and even Kemble's own *Journal of a Residence*, to say nothing of Alexis de Tocqueville. As travelers' accounts go, this journal remains sufficiently impressionistic to permit us to wonder about its author's intentions.

Although we are accustomed to think of journals and diaries as essentially personal and even confessional, Kemble's steadfastly eschews the confessional mode. Here and there, she writes of her personal responses, but only of the most neutral: her responses to discomfort, her judgments of others' behavior, and once her personal experience of fear. Pierce Butler, whom she would marry in the very month (June 1834) in which the journal leaves off, figures with increasing frequency in it from 1833 on, but he receives no personal comment at all. Kemble does not even tell us that he is so constantly mentioned during its closing months because he has fallen in love with Fanny and has accompanied the Kembles on their tour, although she does, again without special comment, show that he accompanies her on unchaperoned expeditions. The reader is given no hint that he and Fanny are planning to marry.

Kemble remains similarly reticent on other personal matters, especially her own inmost feelings. Her journal, in this respect, does not belong to the recognized genre of confessional self-exploration. If anything, this uncommonly talented and poised twenty-three-year-old takes herself as given. Her journal of an actual journey never moves into the realm of metaphor—the journey to self-knowledge. She never confides in her readers, never entrusts us with her secrets. At most, she tersely notes that she did or did not act well on this or that evening.

Reticence notwithstanding, Kemble's journal is, in essential respects, a self-representation—or, a more correctly, a self-portrait. With three years of success as an actress behind her when she began this journal, Kemble could take herself for granted. Her journal would potentially be of interest because she was who she was—Fanny Kemble. She understandably felt no need to introduce herself to her readers. Nor presumably, did she feel any obligation to revel her private thoughts. Her self-portrait was fashioned less in the interests of candor—much less self-revelation—than in the interests of a subtle and refined self-promotion. Not for her that wanton exhibitionism which would bare the private self to the public gaze. Rather, she sought to construct a public self-representation that would reinforce and enhance her already established reputation as an actress. And she realized her self-appointed task with consummate skill.

The narrator—or self—of Kemble's journal emerges as a cultivated, tasteful, and refined English observer of the American scene. Throughout the journal, Kemble makes scant reference to herself, says little that would remind her readers that she is an unmarried young woman of twenty-three. Her self-representation emerges primarily from her observations on and responses to others, and especially to American manners and morals. Her principal self-identification emerges from her contrasting England and America, from her abiding nostalgia for the England she has left. Although she regularly refers to her own performances at various theaters, she otherwise writes little of her position as an actress.

Kemble established herself as a recognized actress during a period in which it was just becoming acceptable for reputable women to perform in public. To be sure, her own aunt, the celebrated Mrs. Siddons, had paved the way in earning a reputation as a brilliant and highly respectable actress. But her success remained exceptional in an age in which most British actresses belonged to troupes that toured the country and enjoyed questionable reputations for morality. The bourgeois public reacted against what it increasingly perceived as eighteenth-century excesses of self-display. During Kemble's lifetime, the reaction took shape as full-blown Victorian domestic prudery and made women's public self-display yet more problematic. In several places, Kemble writes of the accomplishments of actors, notably her own father and Edmund Kean, in a manner that underscores the artistry and skill of their craft. But she mentions no other actresses at all. In a serious discussion of the best way to stage the witches' scene in *Macbeth,* she refers in passing to the actors who were (mis)playing them, thus, if unintentionally, reminding her readers that many female roles were still being performed by men.

Parts of the journal suggest that Kemble may have been concerned to establish the legitimacy of her own appearance on the stage and, especially, her own credentials as a respectable woman, although she never explicitly raises the issue. In fact, on more than one occasion she takes pains to underscore the artifice of the theatrical performance. She regularly comments on her own performance, sometimes judging it good, sometimes poor. She readily points out the absurd reality that underlies the illusion of the play, ridiculing, for example, a performance during which a costume that was too small for her kept ripping as she moved. She ruthlessly dissects inferior and even comically bad renditions of *Romeo and Juliet*, the play in which she had scored her own first success, which she still loves, and cannot bear to have performed incompetently. In a more general way, she reflects that acting is the lowest of the arts—if it is indeed an art at all. Should it not, she wonders, thus undercutting her own status as an actress, more properly be viewed as a mere amusement?

In these and other ways, Kemble carefully refrains from taking herself as actress too seriously and subtly distances herself from the condition of actress. Yet she is fully capable of covertly defending the profession of acting as craft and even, implicitly, as art. In particular, she fiercely links acting to Shakespeare, the greatest embodiment of English literature. Time and again she refers to the beauty and genius of Shakespeare's plays, berating those who betray their sublime integrity by poor acting. She thereby covertly associates those who act them well with their intrinsic worth. Driving home the relation between fine acting and literary genius, she forcefully opposes the idea advanced by one of her acquaintances that drama could best be rendered by having individuals recite key monologues in private social gatherings. Not possible, she fumes. Shakespeare so rendered would be Shakespeare denatured. Even his eternal lines depend for their full beauty and meaning upon the enactment of the entire play—the stage, the sets, the costumes, the actors.

Kemble's ambiguities and inconsistencies about acting doubtless testify to some uncertainty about her own status as a professional actress. The studied objectivity with which she treats the topic in general and her own performances in particular further emphasizes the distance she seeks to establish between herself and her public role, as does her repeated association of the theater and acting with men. On her telling, her role as an actress represents nothing more or less than her practice of a craft. She never claims any special talent or consideration as a woman and so, by the same token, makes no apology for engaging in what some might view as unwomanly self-display.

The publication of this journal and other evidence confirm that Kemble harbored no serious doubts about her right as a woman to enter the public sphere. Her most cherished ambitions concerned writing for publication rather than acting, which she had taken up primarily to help her family's financial situation. Even before she went on the stage, she had written a play, *Francis I.* Most of her difficulties with her husband, Pierce Butler, apparently stemmed from her unwillingness to accept the subservient role of wife that he considered essential. Her determination to publish this journal gave rise to a protracted quarrel that was never smoothed over and that must be recognized as one of the contributing causes of their divorce. But the journal does not openly testify to Kemble's commitment to the independent rights of women, nor does it openly emphasize her personal claims to consideration and respect.

Kemble's standards for her personal merit lie not in her acting, nor even explicitly in her status as writer, but in her nationality, her culture, her breeding, her class, with her nationality invariably surpassing and informing the rest. Above all she is English. From first to last, England affords the standards by which she judges everything American. From first to last England figures as the sign of everything she values.

Throughout the journal, Kemble evokes England as the talisman of her identity. In words disconcertingly similar to those of Robert Browning's "Home Thoughts from Abroad," she voices the nostalgia of the unwilling exile. Oh, to be in England! Oh, to enjoy the English spring! Oh, to smell an English flower! The condition of American roads evokes unflattering comparisons with those of England. The quality of American labor could not be worse; the bearing of American laborers could not be more provocative and insulting. The products of that labor are invariably inferior to English goods. (Thank goodness, Pierce Butler had the wit and consideration to bring some silver forks on the tour in upstate New York, "for the wretched two-pronged iron implements furnished by our host were anything but clean or convenient.") American horses lack any semblance of decent training, but then Americans do not really know how to ride. American women, although beautiful, are insufferably dressed and speak in shrill, grating voices. American men are, in general, hard-driving and coarse. The country's famed republican feeling amounts to a mixture of "impudence and vulgarity to be met with no where but in America." American violets and cowslips have no fragrance. Americans have no sense of that good home religion that anchors any respectable society—do not even regularly celebrate Christmas in the family circle. In short, America is replicating England in caricature, replicating the forms with none of the substance.

Kemble assuredly knew that in sharply criticizing American manners and morals she was establishing herself as superior to Americans. And the qualities in which she depicted herself as superior deserve attention. She understood the qualities of a good horse; she appreciated the fragrance of even the humblest flower; she had impeccable taste in fashion; she spoke in a cultured voice; she appreciated the quality of fine workmanship; she expected the appropriate deference from servants; she knew the difference between silver and iron; she knew, above all, what it was to be a lady. And should her readers mistake her deeper meaning, she insists on "what I have always thought most sacred," namely, "the dignity of woman in her own eyes and those of others." Kemble reserved her private responses for her protracted correspondence with her closest friend, Harriet St. Leger. In this journal, she offers us something else: a highly crafted portrait of herself as discriminating observer.

It is hard to believe that Kemble did not, from the outset, keep her journal with a public purpose in mind. As early as the initial trip across the Atlantic, she mentions that she read her journal to her fellow travelers, the Hodgkinsons. Doubtless her lifelong ambition to excel as a writer informed the care with which she recorded discrete incidents and observations. She frequently dwells upon her love for literature, notably Shakespeare and Byron. Washington Irving, whose work she much admired, evokes one of her few admissions of admiration for things American. Writing, in contrast to acting, unquestionably figured as one of the arts. Writing offered an enduring way to establish her own talent.

The superficially episodic and casual style of a journal also offered protection against the naked display of ambition. Presenting herself as observer rather than as protagonist, or even as author in the formal sense, shielded her from accusations of self-promotion or self-display. By the time that she committed her observations to print, she indisputably knew that many, beginning with her own husband, would not accept her protestations of innocence. She even noted that during her stay in Washington the natives had taken her talk as an insult to America and Americans: "All Washington was in dismay, and my evil deeds and evil words was town talk." But by the time she was revising the journal for publication, she was prepared to dismiss all objections as parochial and self-interested. Perhaps the pithiness of her comments on America did provoke narrow

American resentment, but that was their problem not hers. She was already serving the larger interests of truth that she would yet more polemically serve in her *Journal of a Residence*. She was representing the excellence of English taste and, in so doing, representing herself as the embodiment of the English gentlewoman.

This journal concludes abruptly with Kemble's first glimpse of Niagara Falls. Earlier in the journal, she had approvingly reported a conversation with Noah Webster in which he had insisted that he would not try to describe Niagara—that no words could capture its grandeur. Nor does she herself try to do so. As they approached the falls, she was taken with "a perfect frenzy of impatience" so that she could have run the whole remaining way. When they actually arrived near the spot, she sprang from the carriage and rushed along the path "divided only by a thicket from the tumultuous rapids." In a minute, she had passed the thicket and "stood upon Table Rock. Trelawney [one of their traveling companions] seized me by the arm, and without speaking a word, dragged me to the edge of the rapids, to the brink of the abyss. I saw Niagara—Oh God! Who can describe that sight!!!" And so concludes the journal, leaving the reader with the self-consciously romantic picture of Fanny at one with one of the great manifestations of nature.

Fanny Kemble's depiction of her travels in America does not explicitly offer a representation of her internal journey to self-knowledge. One is even permitted to speculate that the published version reflects an uneasy compromise between the self that experienced those travels and the self that published their account. For during the years of the journal, Kemble was falling in love and deciding to marry. By the time she was revising for publication, her marriage was in trouble and her determination to publish was adding to other difficulties. Her representation of herself embodies something of both selves and, in attempting to compromise between them, emphasizes what she wished to be viewed as the constant features of her character. The journal, in this respect, offers a static rather than a dynamic self-representation. It also offers a remarkable, if oblique, glimpse of the mind of an extraordinary woman.

Elizabeth Fox-Genovese
Emory University

PREFACE

Frances Anne Kemble—always known as "Fanny"—was born in London on November 29, 1809. Her mother, of French-Swiss origin, had been a ballet dancer before her marriage to Charles Kemble, one of the twelve children of the well-known strolling player, Roger Kemble. Other members of the family included the distinguished actor and theater manager, John Philip Kemble, and the great Sarah Siddons.

Fanny's parents were determined that their lively little daughter would never go on the stage, and she was given an excellent education in France. By the time she left school, aged 16, she was fluent in French and Italian, and had achieved a good standard in singing, dancing, and the piano.

While staying with one of her aunts, she met Harriet St. Leger, a spinster Irish lady of independent means, who became Fanny's regular correspondent for many years.

Charles Kemble had taken over the management of the Theatre Royal, Covent Garden (as it was then called) on the death of his brother, John Philip Kemble in 1823. But he was no businessman, and by 1829 the theater was in serious financial trouble, and Charles about to be declared bankrupt.

After much family discussion, it was decided that perhaps Fanny could save the day. Accordingly, with no training and after only three weeks rehearsal, Fanny made her debut as Juliet at Covent Garden on October 5, 1829. Overnight a star was born! The theater was packed each night she appeared, and members of the aristocracy came to her dressing room with congratulations and invitations.

A very successful provincial tour with her father followed in the summer of 1830, another London season in the autumn into spring 1831, and then more touring. Everywhere the Kembles went they were enthusiastically received.

But in spite of all this, more financial trouble at Covent Garden was looming. This time Charles' solution was more drastic—he would sell up, and, with Fanny, seek their fortunes in America.

Fanny played at Covent Garden for the last time on June 22, 1832, and she wrote to her friend, Harriet St. Leger: "It made by heart ache to leave my kind, good, indulgent audience, my friends, my English folk."

On August 1, 1832, Charles and Fanny left England for America. With them went Fanny's aunt Adelaide—always known as "Dall." She had made her home with Fanny's family after an unhappy love affair in her youth, and during the tour, was a tower of strength to her niece, till her tragic death in Boston in 1834.

When they were playing in Philadelphia in October 1832, a young man called at the Kembles' hotel, and made himself very agreeable to Fanny. Throughout the tour Pierce Butler was always around, making himself useful, and eventually Fanny and Pierce Butler fell in love, and were married in Philadelphia in July 1834.

By this time Fanny had finished her journal, and had an offer for publication from Carey, Lea & Blanchard of Philadelphia. But Pierce did not care for the idea of his wife publishing a book, and making her own money, so he tried bribing the publisher not to bring it out. When this was unsuccessful, Pierce went through his wife's manuscript and crossed out all the names of the people she had mentioned. So the *Journal* came out in 1835, with each page full of initials and dashes—"When we got back from the theatre, Mr. D.——— was waiting for us"—and so on.

I was given a copy of the *Journal* some years ago, bought at auction in New York, and at once realized its great interest, but also that no modern publisher would consider it with all those initials and dashes. However, I discovered that a copy with all the names filled in by Fanny, was held in the Rare Books Department of Columbia University Library, donated by one of her friends. By courtesy of the Librarian of that department, Kenneth A. Lohf, I was able to obtain a microfilm of the *Journal,* fill in the names, and prepare a modern edition.

So now, through the courtesy of the Columbia University Press, I am able to offer to readers in the United States and the United Kingdom this fascinating journal, written by the young English actress during the tour with her father from 1832 to 1834.

Monica Gough

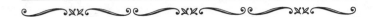

ACKNOWLEDGMENTS

The following have helped me tremendously throughout my work on Fanny Kemble, both in practical ways, and with encouragement and moral support: Kathleen Barker, Alan Cuckston, Giles Havergal, Lucyle Hook, Gillian Hush, Kenneth A. Lohf, James Lomax, Margaretta Scott, and David Woodcock.

I would also like to thank my good friend and literary agent, Patsy Fraser, and to acknowledge the interest and encouragement of Jennifer Crewe, executive editor at Columbia University Press.

FANNY KEMBLE

Journal of a Young Actress

I

Bound for America—Fellow passengers—Stormy weather—
Land! Land!

Wednesday, August 1st, 1832

ANOTHER break in my journal and here I am on board
the *Pacific*, bound for America, having left home and
all the world behind—Well! We reached the quay just as
the ship was being pushed and pulled and levered to the
entrance of the dock. The quays were lined with people
among whom were several known faces, who came on board
to take my letters and bid us goodbye.

I had a bunch of carnations in my hand, which I had
snatched from our drawing-room chimney—English flowers! dear English flowers! they will be withered long before
I see land again, but I will keep them until I once more
stand upon the soil on which they grew.

The sky had become clouded and the wind blew cold.
Came down and put our narrow room to rights. Worked at
my Bible cover till dinner time. We dined at half past three.
The table was excellent, cold dinner because it was the first
day—but everything was good—champagne and dessert and
every luxury imaginable, rendered it as little like a ship-
dinner as maybe. The man who sat by me was an American, very good-natured and talkative. Our passengers are
all men, with the exception of three; a nice pretty-looking
girl who is going out with her brother, a fat old woman and

1

a fat young one. I cried almost the whole of dinner time.

After dinner the ladies adjourned to their own cabin, and the gentlemen began to debate about regulating the meal hours. They adopted the debating society tone, called my dear father to the chair, and presently I heard—oh horror! (what I had not thought to hear again for six weeks) the clapping of hands. They sent him in to consult us about dinner hour, and we having decided four o'clock, the debate continued with considerable merriment. Presently my father, Colonel Sibell and Mr. Hodgkinson came into our cabin, and the former read us Washington Irving's speech at the New York dinner. Some of it is very beautiful, all of it is in good feeling—it made me cry. Oh my home, my land, my England, glorious little England! I sat working till the gentlemen left us, and then wrote my journal. I am weary and sad, and will try to go to sleep—it rains, I cannot see the moon.

Thursday, August 2nd

IT rained all night and in the morning the wind had died away, and we lay rocking becalmed on the waveless waters. At eight o'clock they brought us some breakfast, after which I got up. While dressing I could not help being amused at hearing the cocks crowing, the cows lowing and ducks gabbling, as though we were in the midst of a farmyard. Having finished my toilet, I emerged, and Miss Hodgkinson and I walked upon the deck. The sea lay grey and still, a sheet of lead, the sky was the same dull colour and the deck was wet and comfortless. The whole was melancholy and sadder than all, sat a poor woman dressed in mourning in a corner of the deck. She was a steerage passenger, and I never saw so much sorrow in any face. Poor thing, her heart was aching for home and kindred left behind her, and it made mine ache to look at her.

Miss Hodgkinson and I walked up and down for an hour. I like my companion well; she is a nice quiet young thing, just come from a country home. Came down and began getting out books for my German lesson, but turning rather awful, left my learning on the floor, and betook myself to my birth [sic]. Slept till nearly dinner time—took my place at table, but presently the misery returned, and getting up while I had sufficient steadiness left to walk becomingly down the room, I came to my cabin. My dinner followed me thither, and lying on my back, I very comfortably discussed it. Later I got up, devoured some raspberry tart and grapes, and being altogether delightful again, sat working and singing till tea-time.

Friday, August 3rd

DRESSED and came on deck. The day was lovely, the sea one deep, dark sapphire, the sky bright and cloudless, the wind mild and soft, too mild to fill our sails, which hung lazily against the masts. Walked on deck with Miss Hodgkinson and Captain Whaite. The latter is a very good-natured, intelligent person, rough and bluff and only seven and twenty, which makes him having command of the ship rather an awful consideration. Presently we were summoned by the sound of a bell and oyez!—oyez!—oyez!—and a society was established for the good demeanour and sociability of the passengers. My father was in the chair. Mr. James Bell was voted secretary. A badge was established, rules and regulations laid down, a code framed, and much laughter and merriment ensued. After dinner, went on deck again, and took a brisk walk with Captain Whaite.

3

Wednesday, August 15th

SOMEBODY asked me if I had any of Mrs. Siddons' hair, so I sent for my dressing box, and forthwith it was overhauled by half the company, whom a rainy day had reduced to a state worse than usual want of occupation. The rain continued all day, and we ladies dined in the round house, where the Captain and Colonel Sibell joined us, and began drinking champagne and induced us to do the same. Afterwards they fell to singing and while they did so, the sky darkened; the rain came pelting down, the black sea swelled and rose, and broke upon the ship's sides into boiling furrows of foam, that fled like ghosts along the inky face of the ocean. The ship scudded before the blast and we managed to keep ourselves warm by singing.

Thursday, August 16th

ROSE at about half past eight, and as soon as our tent was spread after breakfast, went on deck and took a longish walk with Mr. Hodgkinson—I like him very much. Gossiped till lunch-time and then took up *Childe Harold*. I thought of dear Harriet. She admires Byron more than I do, and yet how wildly I did, how deeply I do still worship his might, majesty and loveliness. After dinner, I and Mr. Bell took a long walk on deck, talking flimsy morality and philosophy. The day was bright and bitter cold, the sea blue and transparent with a lining of pearly foam and glittering spray that enchanted me.

Friday, August 17th

ON my back all day—the ship reeled about like a drunken thing. I lay down and began reading Byron's life. Had he been less of an egoist would he have been so great a poet? I question it. I wonder Byron was moved by criticism. I should have thought him at once too highly armed and too self-wrapped to care for it. Ate nothing but figs and raisins. In the evening some of our gentlemen came into our cabin and sat with us. I in very desperation and sea-sickness began embroidering one of my nightcaps, wherein I persevered till sleep overtook me.

Saturday, August 18th

ROSE about half past eight, dawdled about as usual, and read a few more pages of Byron's life. After breakfast got Colonel Sibell to read *Quentin Durward* to us as we sat working under our canvas pavilion. Our company consists chiefly of traders in cloth and hardware, clerks and counting-house men. Most of them have crossed this trifling ditch half a dozen times in the course of their various avocations. Mr. Hodgkinson read to us after lunch, and we sat happily under our awning till the rain drove us in. Our main-top gallant mast had been split in one of our late blows, and I went out in the rain to see them restore the spar. Towards evening the wind freshened and our gentlemen's spirits rose, and soon, in spite of the rain, they were dancing and singing and romping like mad things. Mr. Bell and I sang through the whole volume of Moore's melodies, and at ten o'clock we adjourned to the gentlemen's cabin to drink to "sweethearts and wives" according to sailors' approved practice.

Sunday, August 19th

DRESSED and came on deck—the morning was brilliant. I amused myself with finding the lessons and collects and psalms for the whole ship's company. After lunch, they spread our tent, a chair was placed for my father, and a little bell being rung, we collected in our rude church. It affected me much, this praying on the lonely sea, in words that at the same hour were being uttered by millions of kindred tongues in our dear home. Oh how I felt all this as we spoke aloud that touching invocation—"Almighty God, who hast promised that when two or three are gathered together in Thy name"—etc. The bright cloudless sky and glorious sea seemed to respond in their silent magnificence to our Te Deum—'twas good—oh! very, very good!

Monday, August 20th

CALM, utter calm—a roasting August sun, a waveless sea, the sails flapping idly against our mast. Wrote my journal, walked about and in the evening danced merrily, quadrilles and country dances. Fairly danced myself tired and came to bed. But oh! not to sleep—mercy what a night! The wind blowing like mad, the ship pitching, bouncing, shuddering, creaking and groaning, till ten o'clock, when I got up and was going to see how near drowning we were, when Dall, who was lying awake too, implored me to lie down again. Lay till daylight, the gale was increasing furiously, boxes, chairs, beds and their contents rolling about in glorious confusion.

Wednesday, August 22nd

A FAIR wind, a fair day—though very very cold and damp. The only one of our crew I cotton on to fairly are the Hodgkinsons and that good-natured lad, Mr. Staley. Though the former rather distress me by their abundant admiration, and the latter by his inveterate Yorkshire, and never opening his mouth when he sings, which, as he has a very sweet voice, is a cruel piece of selfishness, keeping half his tones and all his words for his own private satisfaction.

Thursday, August 23rd

A FINE day, walked about, wrote journal, read some of it to the Hodgkinsons, who seemed much gratified by my doing so. I go on with Byron's life. He is too much of an egoist. I think I never read anything professing to be a person's undisguised feelings and opinions with so much heartlessness, so little goodness in it. Dined at table again. They abound in toasts, and among others, gave "the friends we have left and those we are going to!" My heart sank. I am going to no friend, and the "stranger" with which the Americans salute wayfarers through their land, is the only title I can claim. After dinner, danced and saw the sun sink in a bed of gorgeous stormy clouds.

Friday, August 24th

ROSE late after a fair night's sleep, and after breakfast read a canto of Dante, when—"A sail! a sail!" was cried from all quarters. Remembering my promise to dear Harriet, I got together my writing materials and scrawled her a few lines. The vessel bore down rapidly upon us, but as there was no prospect of either her or us lying to, Mr. Hodgkinson tied my missive, together with one he had just scribbled, to a lump of lead, and presently we all rushed on deck to see the ship pass us. She was an English packet, from Valparaiso, bound for London, and as she passed us, Mr. Hodgkinson got up into a boat to have a better chance of throwing. I saw him fling powerfully, the little packet whizzed through the air, but the distance was impossible. The dark waters received it within twenty feet of the ship, which sailed rapidly on and soon left us far behind. I believe I screamed as the black sea closed over my poor letter. Came down to my cabin and cried like a wretch. After dinner had a sick headache, and walked on deck. The wind and the sea were both rising, the sky had grown mirk as midnight, and the wind that came rushing over the sea was hot from the south. At tea, the crazy old ship in one of her headlong bounces, flung my whole supper in my lap. The wind and water were riotous and the whole ship plunged and shuddered.

Wednesday, August 28th

A MISERBLE day spent between heart-ache and side-ache. The Captain today brought me a land-swallow, which having flown out so far, came hovering over the ship and suffered itself to be caught. Poor little creature! I felt sad for its weary little wings and frightened heart which beat against my hand. I made a cage in a basket for it and gave it some seed, which it will not eat, carniverous little wretch!—I must catch some flies for it.

Thursday, August 29th

MY poor little bird is dead. Poor little creature! I wish it had not died—I would have borne it tenderly and carefully to shore, and given it back to the air again.

Friday, August 30th

A FOG and calm. Sky yellow, sea grey, dripping, dark, damp, and very disagreeable. Sat working, reading and talking in our cabin all day. Its too hard to be becalmed within thirty hours of our destination.

BECALMED again till about two o'clock, when a fair wind sprang up and we set to rolling before it like mad. Got very sick and lay on the ground till dinner time. Went to table but withdrew while it was still in my power to do so gracefully. It suddenly occurred to me that it was our last Saturday night on board. Last—last—what is there in that word? I don't know one of the ship's company, don't care for some of them—I have led a loathsome life in it for the past month, and yet the *last* Saturday night seemed sad to me. Came to bed at about half past twelve, and while undressing, I heard the Captain announce that we were clear of Nantucket shoal, and within one hundred and fifty miles of New York, which intelligence was received with three cheers.

September 1st, Sunday

ROSE at half past six, went on deck, the sun was shining brilliantly. The morning was glorious, the sun had risen two hours ago, the sea was cut by a strong breeze, and curled into ridges that came like emerald banks crowned with golden spray round our ship. After breakfast put my things to rights and while doing so, the joyful sound—"Land! land!" was heard aloft. I rushed on deck and between the blue waveless sea and the bright unclouded sky, lay the wished-for line of a darker element. 'Twas Long Island. Hail, strange land! my heart greets you coldly and sadly! The day was heavenly, though intensely hot, the sky utterly cloudless. They tell me that this is their American weather almost till Christmas—that's nice, for those who like frying. Commend me to dear England's soft, rich, harmonious skies and foliage, commend me to the misty curtain of silver vapour that hangs over her September woods at morning, and shrouds them at night—in short—I am homesick before touching land.

We were talking today to one of our steerage passengers, a Huddersfield manufacturer, going out in quest of a living, with five children of his own to take care of, and two nephews. The father of the latter, said our Yorkshireman, having married a second time, and these poor children being as it were, thrust into the world—"why, I just took care of them". Verily, verily, he will have his reward—these tender mercies of the poor to one another are beautiful and most touching.

September 2nd, Monday

I HAD desired the mate to call me by sunrise, and accordingly in the midst of a very sound sleep, Mr. Curtis shook me roughly by the arm, informing me that the sun was just about to rise. I called Harriet, and we remained on deck watching the clouds like visions of brightness and beauty, at every moment assuming more fantastic shapes and gorgeous tints. Oh, it was surpassing! We were becalmed, however, which rather damped all our spirits, and made the Captain swear. Towards midday we had to thank heaven for an incident. A brig had been standing aft against the horizon for some hours past, and we presently descried a boat rowing towards us from her. The distance was some five miles, they rowed stoutly and in due time boarded us. She was an English brig from Bristol, had been out eleven weeks, distressed by contrary winds and was in want of provisions. Our dear Captain supplied them with everything they wanted, and the poor steerage passengers sent their mite to the distressed crews in the shape of the sack of potatoes. After this the whole day was one of continual excitement. At about four o'clock, a schooner came alongside with a news collector—he was half devoured with questions, news of the cholera, reports of the tariff and bank questions were loudly demanded. Poor people, how anxiously they looked for replies to the first. Mr. Hodgkinson turned as pale as death while asking how it had visited Boston.

Poor fellow! poor people! my heart ached for their anxiety. As the evening darkened, the horizon became studded with sails. At about eight o'clock we discovered the Highlands of Neversink, the entrance to New York harbour, and presently the twin lights of Sandy Hook glimmered against the sky. We were all in high spirits, a fresh breeze had sprung up, and the Captain alone seemed anxious, eagerly looking out for the pilot. Some had gathered at the ship's side, to watch the progress of Colonel Sibell, who had left us to go into the newsboat, which was dancing by the side of our dark vessel. Cheering resounded on all sides, rockets were fired from the ship's stern, we were all dancing, when suddenly a cry echoed round—"A pilot! a pilot!", and close under the ship's side a light graceful little schooner shot like an arrow through the dim twilight. She tacked and lay to, but proved to be only another newsboat. While we were all gathered round, the pilot-boat came alongside, with the pilot on board. The Captain gave up the cares and glories of command and we danced an interminable country dance. All was excitement and joyous confusion. Poor Mr. Bell alone seemed smitten with sudden anxiety. The cholera reports had filled him with alarm, lest his agent should have died, and his affairs on arrival be in confusion and ruin—poor fellow, I was very sorry for him. We went down to supper at ten, and were very merry, in spite of the ship's bumping once or twice upon the sands. Came up and saw them cast anchor, away went the chain, down dropped the heavy stay, the fair ship swung round, and there lay New York before us, with its clustered lights shining like a distant constellation against the dark land. Our cradle rocks no longer, but lies on the still waters. We have reached our destination—thank God! I did so with all my soul.

II

Arrival in New York—First impressions—Walking in New York

Tuesday, September 3rd

OUR passengers were all stirring and about at peep of day, and I got up myself at half past six. Trunks lay scattered in every direction around, and all were busily preparing to leave the good ship *Pacific*. Mercy on us! it made me sad to leave her and my shipmates. The morning was real Manchester. A fog hung over the shores of Staten Island and Long Island, in spite of which, and a dreary, heavy, thick rain, I thought the hilly outline of the former very beautiful. We breakfasted, packed ourselves into our shawls and bonnets, and at half past nine the steamboat came alongside to take us to the shore. We got on board her all in rain and misery, and as we drifted on, our passengers collected to the side of the boat, and gave three cheers. Poor ship! there she lay—all sails reefed, rocking in melancholy inaction deserted by her merry inmates, lonely and idle—poor *Pacific!* All were looking at the shores, some wondering and admiring, others recognising through the rain and mist as they might. I could not endure to lift my eyes to the strange land, and even had I done so, was crying too bitterly to see anything. Mr. Hodgkinson and Mr. Staley went to secure apartments for us at the American Hotel, and after bidding goodbye to the sea, we packed ourselves

13

into a hackney coach and progressed. The houses were almost all painted pale straw colour and grey. They all have green Venetian shutters, which give an idea of coolness and almost every house has a tree or trees in its vicinity, which looks pretty and garden-like. We reached our inn, the gentlemen were waiting for us, and led us into our drawing-room. I had been choking for the last three hours, and could endure no more, but sobbed like a wretch aloud.

There was a piano in the room, to which I flew with the appetite of one who has lived on the music of the speaking-trumpet for a month. That, and some iced lemonade, presently restored my spirits.

At five o'clock we all met at dinner. Our drawing-room being large and pleasant the table was laid in it. Our dinner was a favourable specimen of eating as practised in this new world. Everything good, only in too great profusion, the wine drinkable and fruit beautiful to look at. In point of flavour it was infinitely inferior to English hothouse fruit, or even good espalier fruit raised in a good aspect. Everything was wrapped in ice, which is a most luxurious necessity in this hot climate. But the things were put on the table in a slovenly outlandish fashion, fish, soup and meat all at once, and puddings and tarts and cheese, all at once. No finger glasses, and a patched table cloth—in short, a want of that style and neatness which is found in every hotel in England. The day had cleared and become intensely hot, towards evening softening and cooling under the serene influence of the loveliest moon imaginable. The streets were brilliantly lighted, the shops through the trees and the people parading between them, reminded me very much of the Boulevards. We left the gentlemen and went downstairs where I played and sang for three hours.

I HAVE been in a sulky fit half the day, because people will keep walking in and out of our room without leave or license. I am delighted to see my friends, but I like to tell them so, and not that they should take it for granted. When I made my appearance in my dressing gown (my clothes not yet come, and the day too hot for a silk pelisse), great was my amazement to find our whole ship's company assembled at the table. After breakfast they dispersed, and I sat writing my journal, and playing and singing.

Mrs. Bioni, my mother's youngest sister called to see Dall. I remember her name as one of the first things I do remember. A visit from William Price, brother to the proprietor of the Park Theatre, and a lawyer of considerable reputation here. We dined at half past two with the Hodgkinsons and Mr. Staley, and then we walked down to the quay to convey them to their steamboat. We saw them on board, and bade our new friends goodbye, and walked briskly to the Battery to see them as they passed it. This Battery is a beautiful marine parade, commanding the harbour and the entrance to the bay, with Governor's Island and its dusky red fort and the woody shores of New Jersey and Long Island. A sort of public promenade formed of grass plots, planted with a variety of trees, affords a very agreeable position from which to enjoy the lovely view. My companion informed me that this was a fashionable resort some time ago, but owing to its being frequented by the lowest and dirtiest of the rabble, who in this land of liberty roll themselves on the grass, and otherwise annoy the more respectable portion of the promenaders, it has been much deserted lately, and is now only traversed by the higher classes as a thoroughfare. The trees and grass were vividly and luxuriantly green, but the latter grew rank and long, unshorn and untidy. It looked neglected and slovenly.

Came home up Broadway, which is a long street of tolerable width, full of shops, in short, the American Oxford Road, where all the people go to exhibit themselves and examine others. The women I have seen hitherto have all been very gaily dressed, with a pretension to the French style, and a more than English exaggeration of it. They all appear to me to walk with a French shuffle, which, as their pavements are flat, I can only account for by their wearing shoes made in the French fashion, which are enough in themselves to make a waddler of the best walker that ever set foot upon earth.

Came home and had tea, after which my father, Mr. Staley and I crossed the Park (a small bit of grass enclosed in white palings), to the Theatre. Wallack was to act in *The Rent Day*. Mercy how strange it felt as I once more set foot in a theatre—the sound of applause set my teeth on edge. The house is pretty though rather gloomy, well formed, about the size of the Haymarket, with plenty of gold carving and red silk about it, looking rich and warm. The audience was considerable, but all men, scarce, I should think, twenty women in the dress circle, where, as well as in the private boxes, I saw men sitting with their hats on. Wallack played admirably. I had never seen him before, and was greatly delighted with his acting. I thought him handsome, of a rustic kind, the very thing for the part he played, a fine English yeoman.

At the end of the play came home with a tremendous headache—sat gossiping and drinking lemonade. Mr. Bell came in to bid us goodbye—he starts for Baltimore tomorrow. He is a nice, good-tempered young Irishman, with more tongue than brains, but still clever enough. I am sorry that he is going. Remained up till one unpacking goods and chattels. Mercy on me! what a cargo it is! They have treated us like ambassadors, and not one of our one and twenty huge boxes have been touched.

AFTER breakfast began writing to my brother, and while doing so Captain Whaite and Mr. Staley called. I was delighted to see our dear captain again. They sat some time and when they were all gone, finished letter and wrote journal. A cheating German woman came here with some bewitching canezous and pelerines. I chose two that I wanted but she asked a heathen price for them. I do not know how it is to be accounted for, but in spite of much lighter duties, every article of dress, particularly silks, embroideries and all French manufacturers are more expensive here than in England. The extravagance of the American woman in this part of their expenditure is, considering the average fortunes in this country, most extraordinary. They never walk in the street but in the most showy and extreme toilette, and I have known twenty, forty and sixty dollars paid for a bonnet to wear for a morning saunter up Broadway.

We dined at five. After dinner sang and played to my father—"All by the light of the moon." The evening was, as the day had been, lovely, and as I stood by his side at the open window, and saw him inhaling the pure fresh air which he said invigorated and refreshed him, half my regret for this exile melted away. My father is ten years younger since he came here already.

AFTER breakfast, Colonel Sibell came to take leave of us for a few days, as he is going to join his wife in the country. Mr. Staley called and remained some time, and while he was here, the waiter brought me word that a Mr. Hone wanted to see me. I sent down word that my father was out, knowing no such person, but the gentleman persisted in seeing me, and presently in walked a good-looking elderly man, who introduced himself as Mr. Hone. He sat himself down, pottered a little and then went away. When he was gone, Mr. Staley informed me that this was one of *the* men of New York, in point of wealth, influence and consideration. He had been a great auctioneer, but had retired from business, having, among other honours, filled the office of Mayor of New York.

After dinner, as I stood at the window looking at the lovely sky and the brilliant earth, a curious effect of light struck me. Within a hundred yards of each other the Town Hall lay, with its white walls glowing in the sunset, while the tall grey church steeple was turning pale in the clear moonlight. That Town Hall is a white-washed anomaly, and yet its effect is not altogether bad.

My father proposed a walk to us and we accordingly sallied forth. We walked to the end of Broadway, a distance of two miles, and then back again. The evening was most lovely. The moon was lighting up the whole upper sky, but every now and then, as we crossed the streets that led to the river, we caught glimpses of the water and woody banks and the sky that hung over them. After walking nearly a mile up Broadway we came to Canal Street, which is finer and broader than any I have yet seen in New York. At one end of it is a Christian church, copied from some pagan temple or other, which looked extremely well in the full flood of silver light which streamed from Heaven.

The street was very thronged, and I thought the crowd a more civil and orderly one than an English crowd. The men did not jostle or push one another, or tread upon one's feet, or kick down one's shoe heels, or crush one's bonnet into one's face, all of which I have seen done in London streets. There is this to be said—the crowd was abroad merely for pleasure, sauntering along, which is a thing never seen in London. I observed that the young men tonight, invariably made room for the women to pass, and many of them as they drew near us, took the segar [sic] from their mouth, which I thought especially courteous.

They were smoking to a man, except those who were spitting. The shops appear to me to make no show whatever, and will not bear comparison with the brilliant display of the Parisian streets or the rich magnificence of ours. The women dress very much and very much like French women gone mad. They all seem to me to walk horribly ill, as if they wore tight shoes.

Saturday, September 7th

M R. Hone and his daughter called. I like him, he appears very intelligent and the expression of his countenance is clever and agreeable. His daughter was dressed up in French clothes and looked very stiff. However a first visit is an awkward thing, and nothing that isn't thoroughbred ever does it quite well.

Wallack dined with us. What a handsome man he is, but oh! what a without and a within actor! I wonder if I carry such a brand in every limb and look of me—if I thought so I would strangle myself. In an actor there is a ceaseless striving for effect, a straining after points in talking. How odious it is to me. Absolute and unmitigated vulgarity I can put up with. But heaven defend me from the genteel version of vulgarity.

ROSE at eight, and while I was dressing I heard sundry exclamations—"Good God! is it you? How have you been?" I opened the door and saw my uncle. He was Mr. Vincent Decamp, my mother's brother, and lessee of the Theatre Royal in Montreal in Canada.

After breakfast went to church with my father. On our way thither we met Mr. Ogden Hoffman, to whom I have taken a special fancy. He is a very charming and intelligent person, an eminent member of the New York bar, with whom we became acquainted soon after our arrival in this country. He is one of the very few shy people I have met in America, a quality which from its rarity here has attained almost the proportions of a virtue. He is clever, humourous, well-informed, and his unusually modest and gentle manner and low sweet voice were great additions to his unusual talents.

The church we went to is situated half way between the Battery and our hotel. It is like a chapel in the exterior, being quite plain and standing close in between the houses. The interior was perfectly simple. 'Tis long since I heard the church service so well read, with so few vices of pronunciation or vulgarisms of emphasis. Our own clergy are shamefully negligent on this point. The organ and the chanting were very good, and the service is little altered—all prayers for our King, Queen, House of Lords, Parliament etc., of course omitted. In lieu of which they pray for the President and all existing authorities.

Came home, the day was like an oven. Presently a visit from "his honour the Recorder", and a twaddling old lawyer by the name of Graham, and a silent young gentleman, his son. They were very droll. The lawyer talked the most, a little, turnippy-looking man, who called me a "female". Again I had the opportunity of perceiving how thorough a chimera is the equality that we talk of as American. Here they were, talking of their aristocracy and democracy, and I'm sure the way in which the lawyer dwelt upon the Duke of Montrose and Lady Loughborough, would have satisfied me that a Lord or a Lady are just as precious in the eyes of these levellers, as in those of the Lord and Lady-loving John Bull himself. They stayed pottering a long time.

I do nothing but look out of my window all blessed day long. The park (as they entitle the green opposite our window), is so very pretty, and the streets so gay, with their throngs of smartly dressed women, and so amusing with their abundant proportion of black and white caricatures, that I find my window the most entertaining station in the world.

After dinner again sat looking at the blacks parading up and down, most of them in the height of fashion with every colour in the rainbow about them. Several of the black women I saw pass had very fine figures, but the contrast of a bright blue, or pink crepe bonnet, with the black face, white teeth, and the glaring blue whites of the eyes, is beyond description grotesque.

At seven o'clock Dall and I walked out together. The evening was very beautiful, and we walked as far as Canal Street and back. We continued our walk down to the Battery, but just as we reaached it, we had to return as it was tea-time. I was sorry as the whole scene was so lovely. The moon shone full upon the trees and the intersecting walks of the promenade, and threw a bright belt of silver along the water's edge. A building which was once a fort, from which the Americans fired upon our ships, is now turned into a sort of cafe, and was brilliantly lighted with coloured lamps, shining among the trees and reflected in the water.

The whole effect was very pretty and very Parisian. We came home and had tea, after which Mr. Staley came in. He told us that we must not walk at night alone, for that we might get spoken to. A friend of his, seeing us go out without a man, had followed us the whole way, in order to see that nothing happened to us—this was very civil. Played and sang, and strove to make that stupid lad sing, but he was shy and would not open his mouth, even a hair's-breadth.

Monday, September 9th

WHEN my father came home, went with him to call on Mrs. Hone. What I saw of the house appeared to me to be very pretty, and well adapted to the heat of the season. A large and lofty room, paved with Indian matting, and furnished with white divan and chairs, no other furniture encumbering it up. It looked very airy and cool. Our hostess did not put herself out of the way to entertain us, but after the first "how do you do", continued conversing with another visitor, leaving us to the mercies of a very pretty young lady, who carried on the conversation at an average of a word every three minutes. Neither Mr. Hone nor his eldest daughter were at home, the latter however, presently came in, and relieved her sister, and me greatly. We sat the proper time and then came away. This is a species of intercourse I love not, I never practised it in my own blessed land, neither will I here.

After dinner, played and sang till eight, and then walked out with Dall and my father by the most brilliant moonlight in the world. We went down to the Battery. The acquatic Vauxhall was lighted up very gaily, and they were sending up rockets every few minutes, which, shooting athwart the sky, threw a bright stream of light over the water, and falling back in a shower of stars, seemed to sink away before the steadfast shining of the moon, who held high supremacy in heaven. The bay lay like molten silver under her light, and every now and then a tiny skiff emerging from the shade crossed the bright waters, its dark hull and white sails relieved between the shining sea and radiant sky.

Tuesday, September 10th

THIS day week we landed in New York, and this day was its prototype—rainy, dull and dreary, with occasional fits of sunshine—as capricious as a fine lady. At one o'clock my father set off with Colonel Sibell for Hoboken, a place across the water, famous once for duelling, but now the favourite resort of a turtle-eating club, who go there every Tuesday to cook and swallow turtle. The day was as bad as a party of pleasure could expect, nevertheless, my father, at the Colonel's insistence, perservered and went forth, leaving me his card of invitation, which made me scream for half an hour—the wording as follows: "Sir, the Hoboken Turtle Club will meet at the grove for spoon exercise, on Tuesday, the 10th inst. By order of the President".

At four o'clock sent for a hairdresser that I might see in good time that I am not made an object for my first night. He was a Frenchman, and after listening profoundly to my description of the head-dress I wanted, replied, "Madame, la difficulté n'est pas d'exécuter votre coiffure, mais de la bien concevoir". However, he concieved and executed sundry very smooth-looking bows, and on the whole dressed my hair very nicely, but charged a dollar for doing so. Sat working till my father came home at about half past six. His account of the dinner was anything but delightful. To be sure he has no taste for ruralities, and his feeling description of the damp ground, damp clothes, damp trees and damp atmosphere, gave me the rheumatiz, let alone that they had nothing to eat but turtle, and that out of iron spoons!

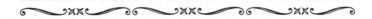

III

Wednesday, September 11th

ROSE at eight and after breakfast, heard my father say Hamlet. How beautiful is his whole conception of the part. I am surprised at anybody's ever questioning the real madness of Hamlet. The entire colour of the character is the proper ground from which to draw the right deduction. Gloomy, despondent, ambitious and disappointed in his ambition, full of sorrow for a dead father, of shame for a living mother, of indignation for his ill-fated inheritance, of impatience at his own dependent position; of a thoughtful, doubtful, questioning spirit, looking with timid boldness from the riddles of earth and life to those of death and the mysterious land beyond it; weary of existence on the very threshold of it, and withheld from self-destruction by religious awe; in love, moreover, and sad and dreamy in his affections. There is not enough of absolute passion in his love to make it a powerful and engrossing interest, and had it been, the truth of Hamlet's character would have been destroyed. Such are the various elements of Hamlet's character at the beginning of the play. Then see what follows. A frightful and unnatural visitation from the dead; a horrible and sudden revelation of the murder of his father, for whom his soul is in morning. Thence, burning hatred and

25

thirst for vengeance against his uncle an imperative duty calling for fulfilment, and a want of resolution and activity to meet the demand. Then comes the vigilant and circumspect guard he is forced to keep upon every word, look and action, lest they reveal his terrible secret, his constant watchfulness over the spies that are set to watch him. Then come, in the course of events, Polonius' death, the unintentional work of his own sword, the second apparition of his father's ghost, his banishment to England, the miserable death of poor Ophelia. If all these—the man's own nature, sad and desponding, reasoning and metaphysical, and the nature he acquires from the tutelage of events, bitter, dark, amazed, uncertain—if these do not make up as complete a madman as ever walked between heaven and earth, I know not what does.

Captain Whaite and Mr. Bell called, the former to ask us to come down and see the *Pacific*, poor old lady! After dinner, walked towards the Battery—Mr. Staley joined us. It was between sunset and moonrise, and a lovelier light never lay upon the sea, earth and sky. The horizon was bright orange colour, fading as it rose to pale amber, which died away again into the modest violet colour of twilight. This possessed the sky wholly, except where two or three masses of soft purple clouds floated, from behind which the stars presently winked at us with their bright eyes. The river lay still as death, though there was a delicious fresh air. Tiny boats were stealing like shadows over the water, and every now and then against the orange edge of the sky moved the masts of some schooner. A band was playing in the Castle garden, and not a creature but ourselves abroad to see all this loveliness. Came home at nine, and my father went to the Park Theatre to see a man of the name of Hackett give an American entertainment after Mathew's fashion. I staid at home looking at the moon which was glorious. As I stood watching that surpassing sunset, I would have given it all, gold, purple and all, for a wreath of English fog stealing over the water.

A T eleven Captain Whaite and Mr. Staley called for us, and my uncle Vincent having joined us, we proceeded to the slip, as they call the places where the ships lie. Poor dear *Pacific!* I ran up her side with great glee and rushed down to my berth, and was actually growing pathetic over the scene of my sea sorrows, when Mr. Staley clapped his hands close to me and startled me out of my reverie. The old ship was dressed out in her best, and after sitting for some time in our cabin, we adjourned to the larger one and lunched. Mr. Curtis joined our party—the first mate, a most courteous and obliging person, and we had one or two of the old ship songs. Visited the forecastle, whence I have watched such glorious sunsets. Poor good ship, I wish to heaven my feet were on her deck and her prow turned to the east. I would not care if the devil himself drove a hurricane at our backs.

Visited the fish and fruit markets. It was too late in the day to see either to advantage, but the latter reminded me of Aladdin's treasure. The heaps of peaches, filling with their rich downy balls high baskets ranged in endless rows, painted a bright vermillion colour, which threw a ruddy ripeness over the fruit. The whole scene enchanted me. Vincent, to my horror, bought a couple of beautiful wild wood-pigeons, which he carried home head downwards, in each coat pocket.

The day was bright and beautiful, and my father proposed crossing the river to Hoboken, the scene of the turtle-eating expedition. Himself, Dall, Mr. Staley and I did so accordingly. Steamers go across every five minutes, conveying passengers on foot and horseback, gigs, carriages, carts, anything and everything. The day was lovely and the broad bright river was gemmed with a thousand sails. Away to the right it stretched between richly wooded banks, placid and blue as a lake. We reached the opposite shore and walked. It was nearly three miles from where we landed to the scene of the "spoon-exercise". The whole of our route lay through a beautiful wild plantation, through which trellis-work of varied foliage, we caught exquisite glimpses of the glorious waters, the glittering city, and the opposite banks, decked out in all the loveliest contrast of sunshine and shade.

Many of the trees were new to me, and delighted me with their graceful forms and vivid foliage. The slips of grass ground on the left of our path were the only things that annoyed me. They were so ragged, rank and high—they wanted mowing, and if they had been mowed soft, thick and smooth, like an English lawn, how gloriously the lights and shadows of this lovely sky would fall upon them. Oh England! England! how I have seen your fresh emerald mantle deepen and brighten on a summer's day.

About a hundred yards from the place where they dined on Tuesday, stands a sort of café, a long low, pretty Italian-looking building. The wood is cleared away in front of it, and it commands a lovely view of the Hudson and its opposite shores. Here they might have been sheltered and comfortable, but I suppose it was not the appointed day of the month for eating their dinner within walls, and rather than infringe on an established rule, they preferred catching a cold apiece. The place where they met in the open air is extremely beautiful, except on a rainy day.

My father, Dall and my bonnet sat down in the shade. Mr. Staley and I clambered upon some pieces of rock at the water's edge, whence we looked out over river and land.

We returned to Dall, my father and my bonnet, buffeting with a swarm of mosquitoes, which were a great nuisance. We turned our steps homewards, and we had to rush to meet the steamboat which was just going across. The whole walk reminded me of that part of Oatlands, which, from its wild and tangled woodlands, they call "America".

Friday, September 13th

DROVE all about New York, which more than ever, reminded me of the towns in France. Passed the Bowery Theatre, which is a handsome, finely proportioned building, with a large brazen eagle plastered on the pediment, for all the world like an insurance mark. We passed a pretty house, which Colonel Sibell called an old mansion. Mercy on me and him! Old! I thought of Warwick Castle, of Hatfield, of Chequers, of Hopwood—old! and there it stood, for all the world like one of our own city's yesterday-grown boxes. The woods, waters and hills and skies alone are old here. The works of men are in the very greenness and unmellowed imperfection of youth. But the Americans are not satisfied with glorying in what they are, but are never happy without comparing this, their sapling, to the giant oaks of the old world, and what can one say to that? Is New York like London? No, it is not, but the oak was an acorn once, and New York will surely, if the world holds together long enough, become a lordly city, such as we know of beyond the sea.

Saturday, September 14th

SAT stitching all the blessed day. At five dressed and went to the Hones, where we were to dine. This is one of the first houses here, so I conclude that I am to consider what I see as a tolerable sample of the ways and manners of being and doing of the *best* society in New York. There were about twenty people, the women in a sort of French demi-toilette with bare necks and long sleeves, hair all frizzed out and thread-net handkerchiefs and capes. The whole of which, to my English eye, appeared a strange marrying of incongruities. The younger daughter of our host is beautiful, a young and brilliant likeness of Ellen Tree, but with more refinement. She was much taken up with a youth, to whom, my neighbour at dinner informed me, she was engaged.

The women here, like those of most warm climates, ripen very early and decay proportionally soon. They are, generally speaking, pretty, with good complexions, and an air of freshness, but this I am told is very evanescent. Whereas in England a woman is in the full bloom of health and beauty from twenty to five and thirty, here they scarcely reach the first period without being faded and looking old.

There was a Mr. Dominic Lynch, the magnus Apollo of New York, who is a musical genius. He sings as well as any gentleman need sing, pronounces Italian well, and accompanies himself without any false chords. All of which renders him *the* man round whom the women listen and languish. He sang the "Phantom Bark"—the last time I heard it was from the lips of Moore, with two of the loveliest faces in all the world hanging over him—Mrs. Norton and Mrs. Blackwood, now Lady Dufferin.

The dinner was plenteous and tolerably well dressed, but ill-served. There were not half enough servants, and we had neither water glasses nor finger glasses. Now though I don't eat with my fingers, yet I do hold a finger glass at the conclusion of my dinner, a requisite comfort. After dinner we had coffee, but no tea, whereat my English taste was in high dudgeon. The gentlemen did not sit long, and when they joined us, Mr. Dominic Lynch, as I said before, uttered sweet sounds. I was not a little amused at Mrs. Hone asking me whether I had heard of his singing or their musical soirées, and seeming surprised that I had no revelations of either across the Atlantic. Mercy on me! what fools people are all over the world! The worst is, they are fools of the same sort, and there is no profit whatever in travelling. Mr. Bancroft, who is an Englishman, happened to ask if I knew Captain Whaite, whereupon we immediately struck of a conversa tion, and talked over English folk and doings, to my entire satisfaction.

I sang to them two or three things, but the piano was pitched too high for my voice. In that large, lofty, fine room, they had a tiny old-fashioned becurtained cabinet piano struck right against the wall, into which the singer's face was turned, and into which his voice was absorbed. We had hardly regained our inn, when in walked Mr. Bancroft to ask if we would not join him and the Cornwalls at supper. He said that besides five being a great deal too early to dine, he had not had half enough dinner. And then began the regular English quizzing of everything and everybody we had left behind. Oh dear! how thoroughly English it was! Of course we did not accept their invitation, but it furnished me a matter of amusement. How we English folk do cling to our own habits, our own views, our own things, our own people.

IV

Charles Kemble's debut as Hamlet—Fanny's debut as Bianca in
Fazio—Shopping in New York—Disaster in Venice Preserved

Monday, September 16th

ROSE at eight, at twelve went to rehearsal. That washed-
out man who failed in London when he acted Romeo
with me is to be my Fazio. Let us hope that he will know
some of his words tomorrow night, for he is at present in-
nocent of any such knowledge. After rehearsal walked into
a shop to buy some gauze. The shopman called me by name,
entered into conversation with us, and one of them, after
showing me a variety of things I did not want, said that
they were anxious to show me every attention, and render
my stay in this country aggreable. For my own part, though
I had the grace to smile and say "thank you", I longed to
add, "but be so good as to measure your ribands and hold
your tongue". I have no idea of holding parley with clerks
behind a counter, still less of their doing so with me. I should
have been better pleased if they had called me "Ma'am",
which they did not.

We dined at three. Vincent and Colonel Sibell called
after dinner, and at seven we went to the theatre. It was
my dear father's first appearance in this new world, and my
heart ached with anxiety. The weather was intensely hot,
yet the theatre was crowded. When he came on, they gave
him what everybody here calls an immense reception, but

they should see our London audience get up and wave hats and handkerchiefs, and shout welcome, as they do to us. The tears were in my eyes, and all I could say was—"They might as well get up, I think". My father looked well and acted beyond all praise. I think it is impossible to conceive Hamlet more truly, or execute it more exquisitely than he does. The refinement, the tenderness, the grace, dignity and princely courtesy with which he invests it from beginning to end, are most lovely. His voice was weak from nervousness and the intolerable heat, and he was not well dressed, which was a pity. The play was well got up, and went off very well. The Hones were there, a regiment of them, also Colonel Sibell and Captain Martin.

Tuesday, September 17th

AT eleven went to rehearsal. Mr. Keppel is just as nervous and as imperfect as ever. What on earth will he or I do tonight? Came home and got things out for the theatre. Mr. Hone and his nephew called. The latter asked me if I was at all apprehensive? No, by my troth, I am not. The whole thing is too loathsome to me for either failure or success to affect me in the least.

At half past six went to the theatre. They acted the farce of *Popping the Question* first, in order, I suppose, to get people to their seats before the play began. Poor Mr. Keppel was gasping for breath. I consoled and comforted him all I could, and gave him some of my lemonade to swallow, for he was choking with fright, then sat myself down with my back to the audience, and up went the curtain. Owing to the position in which I was sitting, and my plain dress, the people did not know me, and would not have known me for some time, if that stupid man had done as I kept bidding him, gone on. Instead, he stood stock still, looked at me, and then at the audience, thereupon the latter caught an inkling of the truth, and gave me such a reception as I get at Covent Garden every time I act a new part. The house was very full, all the Hones were there, and Colonel Sibell. Mr. Keppel was frightened to death and in the very second speech was quite out. It was in vain that I prompted him, he was too nervous to take the word and made a complete mess of it. This happened more than once in the first scene, and at the end of the first act, as I left the stage, I said to Dall, "It's all up with me, I can't do anything now!" Having to prompt my Fazio, frightened by his fright, annoyed by his forgetting his crossings and positions, I thought the whole thing must necessarily go to pieces.

However, once rid of my encumbrance, which I am at the end of the second act, I began to move a little more freely, gathered up my strength, and set to work comfortably by myself. Whereupon the people applauded, I warmed, and got through very satisfactorily, or so it seems. After the play, my father introduced me to Mr. Berkley, who was behind the scenes. Came home to bed at half past twelve, weary and half melted away. The ants swarm on the floor, on the tables, in the beds, about one's clothes. The plagues of Egypt were a joke to them.

Wednesday, September 18th

AFTER breakfast, went off to rehearsal—*Romeo and Juliet.* Mr. Keppel has been dismissed, poor man! I'm sorry for him. My father is to play Romeo—I'm sorrier still for that. After rehearsal Mr. Berkley called. He is particularly fond of music, and my father asked him to try the piano, and was playing most delightfully when in walked Mr. Hone, followed by Colonel Sibell. At five our dinner party assembled. Our dinner was neither good nor well served, the wine not half iced. At the end of it, my father gave Captain Whaite his claret jug, with which that worthy seemed much satisfied. Then they put me down to the piano, and once or twice I thought I must have screamed. Dear Mr. Bell vibrated at my side, threatening my new gown with a cup of coffee, which he held at an awful angle from the horizontal, singing with everybody who opened their lips, and uttering such dreadfully discordant little squeals and squeaks, that I thought I should have died with suppressed laughter. On the other side, stood the Irishman, who, though warbling a little out of tune, still retained enough of his right senses to discriminate between Mr. Bell's yelps, and singing, properly so-called. They all went away in good time, and we came to bed.

> —to bed—to sleep—
> *To sleep! perchance to be bitten! Aye, there's the scratch;*
> *And in that sleep of ours what bugs may come,*
> *Must give us pause.*

Thursday, September 19th

AFTER breakfast went to rehearse *Romeo and Juliet.* Poor Mr. Keppel is fairly laid on the shelf—I'm sorry for him. What a funny passion he had, by the way, for going down on his knees. In *Fazio*, at the end of the judgement scene, when I was upon mine, down he went upon his, making the most absurd devout looking vis-à-vis I ever beheld. In the last scene too, when he ought to have been going off to execution, down he went again on his knees, and no power on earth could get him up again for Lord knows how long! Poor fellow, he bothered me a great deal, yet I'm sincerely sorry for him.

Mr. Hone called and asked us to dinner tomorrow to meet

Dr. Wainwright, who, poor man, dares neither to go to the play nor to call upon us. So strict are the good people about the behaviour of their pastors and masters. This morning, Essex called to fetch away the Captain's jug. He asked my father for an order, adding, with some hesitation, "It must be for the gallery, if you please, sir, for people of colour are not allowed in the pit, or any other part of the house". I believe I turned black myself, I was so indignant.

At half past six went to the theatre. The house was very full and dreadfully hot. My father acted Romeo beautifully, and I looked very nice and the people applauded my *gown* abundantly. At the end of the play I was half dead with heat and fatigue.

Friday, September 20th

THIS morning, a letter from Mr. Keppel, soliciting another trial, and urging the harshness of his case, in being condemned upon a part which he had had no time to study. My own opinion of poor Mr. Keppel is that no power on earth or in heaven can make him act decently. However, I don't object to his trying again; he did not swamp me the first night, so I don't suppose he will the fifth. Just before dinner received a most delicious bouquet, which gladdened by heart with its sweet smell and lovely colours. Some of the flowers were strangers to me. After dinner, Colonel Sibell called, and began pulling out heaps of newspapers, and telling us a long story about Mr. Keppel, who, it seems, has been writing to the papers to convince them and the public that he is a good actor.

When he had gone, went to the theatre; the house was very good, the play *The School of Scandal*. I played pretty fairly and looked very nice. The people were stupid to a degree, to be sure—poor things, it was very hot. The few critiques I have seen upon our acting have been, on the whole, laudatory. One was sent to me from a paper called *The Mirror*, which pleased me very much. Not because the praise in it was excessive, and far beyond my deserts, but it was written with great taste and feeling, and was not a product of a common press hack.

AFTER breakfast got into a hackney carriage with Dall, and went to a shop to order a pair of shoes. The shopkeepers with whom I have hitherto had to deal, are either condescendingly familiar, or insolently indifferent in their manner. Your washer-woman sits down before you while you are standing to speak to her; a shop boy bringing things for your inspection, not only sits down, but keeps his hat on in your drawing room. The worthy man to whom I went for my shoes was so amazingly ungracious, that at first I thought I would go out of the shop. But recollecting that I should probably go further and fare worse, I gulped, sat down, and was measured.

Came home, and at five went in to our neighbours. Dr. Wainwright, the Rector of Grace Church, was the only stranger. I like him extremely—a charming and intelligent man. His conversation was clever, with an abundance of goodness and liberal benevolent feeling shining through it. We retired to our drawing room, where Mrs. Bancroft made me laugh extremely with sundry passages of her American experiences. I was particularly amused by her account of their stopping, after a long day's journey, at an inn somewhere, where the hostess, who remained in the room the whole time, addressed her as follows—"D'ye play?", pointing to an open pianoforte. Mrs. Bancroft replied that she did sometimes, whereupon the free and easy landlady ordered candles, and added—"Come, sit down and give us a tune then," to which courteous invitation Mrs. Bancroft replied by taking up her candle and walking out of the room. Dr. Wainwright is perfectly enchanting. They left us about eleven, and I went to bed.

Sunday, September 22nd

WENT to church with Dall. The day was most lovely and my eyes were constantly attracted to the church windows, through which the magnificent willows of the burial ground looked like golden-green fountains rising into the sky. The singing was excellent, and Dr. Wainwright's sermon very good too. After church, Mr. Ogden Hoffman called and sat with us during dinner, telling us stories of the flogging of slaves, as he himself had witnessed it in the south. Rage and indignation forced the colour into my face, tears into my eyes, and strained every muscle in my body. He made me perfectly sick with it.

Monday, September 23rd

WENT to rehearsale—*Venice Preserved*, with Mr. Keppel, who did not appear to know the words even and seemed perfectly bewildered at being asked to do the common business of the piece. "Mercy on me! what will he do tonight!", thought I. After dinner, played and wrote my journal and at six went to the theatre. My gown was horribly ill-plaited [sic] and I looked like a blue bag. The house was very full, and they received Mr. Keppel with acclamations and shouts of applause. When I went on, I was all but tumbling down at the sight of my Jaffier, who looked like the apothecary in *Romeo and Juliet,* with the addition of some devilish red slashes along his arms and thighs. The first scene passed well, but oh, the next, and the next, and the next. Whenever he was not glued to my side, he stood three yards behind me. He did nothing but seize my hand and grapple to it so hard, that unless I had knocked him down (which I felt much inclined to try), I could not disengage myself. In the senate scene, when I was entreating for mercy, and struggling, as Otway has it, for my life, he was prancing around the stage in every direction, flourishing his dagger in the air. I wish to heaven I had got up and run away, it would have been natural and served him right. In the parting scene, instead of going away from me when he said, "Farewell for ever!", he stuck to my skirts, though in the same breath that I adjured him in the words of my part not to leave me, I added aside, "Get away from me, oh do!". When I exclaimed "Not one kiss at parting", he kept embracing and kissing me like mad, and when I ought to have been pursuing him, and calling after him, "Leave thy dagger with me!", he hung himself up against the wing, and remained dangling there for five minutes. I was half crazy! The good people sat and swallowed it all. They deserved it, by my troth, they did. I prompted him constantly, and once, after struggling in vain to free myself from him, was obliged in the middle of my part, to exclaim, "You hurt me dreadfully, Mr. Keppel!" He clung to me, cramped me, crumpled me—dreadful! I never experienced anything like this before, and made up my mind I never would again. I played of course like a wretch, finished my part as well as I could, and as soon as the play was over, went to my father and Mr. Simpson and declared to them both my determination not to go upon the stage again with that gentleman for a hero. Come what may, I will not be subjected to this sort of experiment again.

At the end of the play, the clever New Yorkers actually called for Mr. Keppel! And this most worthless clapping of hands, most worthlessly bestowed upon such a worthless object, is what, by the nature of my craft, I am bound to care for. I spit at it from the bottom of my soul! Talking of applause, the man who acted Bedamar tonight thought fit to be two hours dragging me off the stage, in consequence of which I had to scream, "Jaffier! Jaffier!", till I thought I should have broken a blood vessel. On my remonstrating with him about this, he said, "Well, you are rewarded, listen"—the people were clapping and shouting vehemently. This is the whole history of actors and acting. We came home tired and thoroughly disgusted, and found no supper. The cooks, who do not live in the house, but come and do their work, and depart home whenever it suits their convenience, had not thought to stay and prepare any supper for us. So we had to wait for the readiest things that could be procured out of doors for us. At last appeared a cold boiled fowl, and some monstrous oysters. They were well-flavoured but their size displeased me, and I swallowed but one and went to bed.

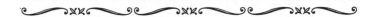

V

Terrible performance of King John—the bazaar-like shops of New York—La Cenerentola at Richmond Hill Theatre

Friday, September 28th

A LETTER from England, the first from dear Harriet. Dall brought it to me while I was dressing, and oh! how welcome it was. Went to rehearsal for *Much Ado About Nothing*. Came home and dined at three. After dinner Ogden Hoffman and Mr. Isaac Hone called and sat with us till six o'clock. I am constantly thunderstruck at the amazing number of questions which people here think fit to ask one, and moreover, expect one to answer.

I would give the world to see Mr. Dominic Lynch directing the public taste, and leading the public approbation, by a gracious tapping of his supreme hand upon his ineffable snuff box. He reminds me of high life below stairs. The play went off very well, I played well and my dresses looked beautiful. My father acted to perfection; I never saw anything so gallant, gay, so like a gentleman, so full of brilliant, buoyant, refined spirit, he looked admirably too. Mr. Berkley was behind the scenes. Speaking to me of my father's appearance as Pierre, he said he reminded him of Lord Dorchester. I could not forbear asking him how long he had been away from England—four years. Truly, four years will furnish him a matter of astonishment when he returns. Swallow Street is grown like a line of palaces; the Strand is

41

a broad magnificent avenue, where all the wealth of the world seems gathered together. Lord Dorchester, the "observed of all observers", is become a fat, red-faced old man.

Monday, October 1st

WHILE I was out, Captain Whaite called for our letters. Then saw Mr. Bancroft, and bade him goodbye, as they are going away today, to La Havre, to Europe. I wish I were a nail in one of their trunks. After breakfast, went to rehearse *King John*—what a lovely mess they will make of it, to be sure. When my sorrows were ended, my father brought me home, and I found a lovely nosegay from Mr. Hone awaiting me. Bless it! how sweet it smelt and how pretty it looked. Spent an hour delightfully putting it into water.

My father received a letter to-day, informing him that a cabal was forming by the friends of Miss Vincent and Miss Clifton (native talent) to hiss us off the New York stage, if possible; if not, to send people in every night to create disturbance during our best scenes. The letter is anonymous, and therefore little deserving of attention.

After dinner practised till time to go to the theatre. The house was very full, but what a cast! what a play! what botchers! what butchers! In the very first scene the most Christian King stuck fast, shifting his truncheon from hand to hand, rolling his eyes, gasping for breath and struggling for words, like a man in a nightmare. I thought of Hamlet, "Leave thy damnable faces", and was obliged to turn away. In the scene before Angiers, when the French and the English heralds summon the citizens to the walls, the Frenchman applied his instrument to his mouth, uplifted his chest, distended his cheeks, and appeared to blow furiously—not a sound! He dropped his arm and looked off stage in discomforture and indignation, when the perverse trumpet set up a blast fit to waken the dead—the audience roared. When Cardinal Pandulph came on, the people set up a shout as usual. He was dreadfully terrified, poor thing, and all the time kept giving little nervous twitches to his sacred petticoat in a fashion that was enough to make one die of laughter. Once, when he stuck fast, having twitched his skirts and thumped his breast in vain for some time, I thought it best having to speak next, to go on. When lo and behold! in the middle of my speech, the scarlet sin recovers his memory, and shouts forth the end of his own to the utter confusion of my august self and of the audience. I thought they would never have got through the last scene. King gazed at Cardinal, and Cardinal gazed at King. King nodded and winked at the prompter, spread out his hands, and remained with his mouth open. Cardinal nodded and winked at the prompter, crossed his hands on his breast, and remained with his mouth open, neither of them uttering a syllable! What a scene! what a glorious scene! I came home as soon as my part was over.

Wednesday, October 2nd

AFTER rehearsal went to Stewart's with Dall. As we were proceeding up Broadway, to Bonfanti's, I saw a man in the strangest attitude imaginable, and who should it be but Mr. Gaston. He came into Bonfanti's with us and afterwards insisting in escorting us to our various destinations—not however without manifold deep lamentations on his slovenly appearance and dirty gloves! The latter, however, he managed to exchange for a pair of new ones, which he extracted from his pocket, and drew on, without letting go of our arms, which he squeezed most unmercifully during the operation!

We went through a part of the town which I had never seen before. The shops have a strange fair-like appearance, and exhibit a spectacle of heterogeneous disorder, which greatly amazed the eye of a Londoner. The comparative infancy in which most of the adornments of life are yet in this country, renders it impossible for the number of distinct trades to exist that do amongst us, where the population is so much denser, and where the luxurious indulgences of the few find ample occupation for the penurious industry of the many. Here, one man follows several trades, and in every shop you meet with a strange incongruous mixture of articles for sale, which would be found nowhere in England, but in the village hucksters. Comparatively few of the objects for sale can be exposed in the windows, which are unlike our shop windows, being narrow and ill-adapted for the display of goods. Piles of them lie outside the doors, choking up the pathway and coloured cloths, flannels, shawls etc. are suspended about in long draperies, whose vivid colours flying over the face of the houses, give them an untidy, but at the same time, a gay flaunting appearance.

We went into a shop to buy some stockings, and missing our gallant chevalier, I turned round to look for him and perceived him beautifying most busily before a glass in a further corner of the shop. He had seized on a brush and began grooming his hat. The next operation was to produce a small pocket comb and arrange his disordered locks. Lastly he transferred the services of the brush of all work from his hat to his feet, and having dusted his boots, drawn himself up in his overcoat and buttoned its two lower buttons, he approached us, evidently much advanced in his own good graces.

AFTER breakfast, went to rehearsal; my Bizarre is getting a little more into shape. After rehearsal, came home, but was called out to look at my gown, which the worthy milliner had sent home. She took it back to alter it. Presently arrived my wreath, and that also had to be taken back, for it was nothing like what I had ordered. Now all this does not provoke me, but the thing that does, is the dreadful want of manners of the trades-people here. They bolt into your room without knocking, nod to you, sit down, and without the preface of either Sir or Madam, or Miss, start off into—"Well now, I'm come to speak about so and so". At six went to the theatre, the play *The Hunchback*. The house was crammed from floor to ceiling. I had an intense headache, but played tolerably well. I wore my red satin and looked like a bonfire. Came home with my head splitting.

PLAYED Bizarre for the first time. Acted so-so, looked very pretty, the house was very full and my father incomparable. They called for him after the play.

ON our way to Mr. Wallack's, my father told me he had been seeing Miss Clifton, the girl they want him to teach to act—to *teach* to act, indeed! He says she is very pretty, with fine eyes, a fair delicate skin and a handsome mouth, moreover, a tall woman, and yet from the front of the house, the effect is nought.

The people here make me mad by abusing Lawrence's

drawing of me. If ever there was a refined and intellectual work, where the might of genius triumphing over every material impediment, has enshrined and embodied spirit itself, it is that. Talking of Lawrence, (poor Lawrence!), Mrs. Hone said—"Ah yes, your picture by—a—Sir—something—Lawrence!" Oh fame! Of vanity and vexation of spirit! does your eternity and your infinitude amount of this! There are lands where Shakespeare's name was never heard, where Raphael and Handel are unknown, and there are regions, (and those wide ones too), where Jesus Christ is unknown.

At nine o'clock went to the Richmond Hill Theatre to see the opening of the Italian company in *La Cenerentola*. The house itself is a pretty little box, but as bad as a box to sing in. We went to Mr. Hone's box, where he was kind enough to give us seats. The first act was over, but we had all the benefit of the second. I had much ado not to laugh, and when Mr. Hoffman, that everlasting giggler came and sat down beside me, I gave myself up for lost! However I did behave myself in spite of two blue bottles of women, who by way of the sisters, buzzed about on the stage, singing enough to set one's teeth on edge.

Then on came a very tall Dandini with a very fine voice. But the Prima Donna! the Cenerentola! what a figure and what a face! Indeed she was the very thing for a lower housemaid, and I think that the Prince was to blame for removing her from the station nature had evidently intended her for. She was old and ugly, unpardonably common-looking, with a cast in her eye, and a foot that, as Mr. Hoffman observed, would require a considerable glass slipper to fit. Then she sang, discords and dismay, how she did sing! I thought of poor dear Adelaide and her sweet voice and her refined taste, and shuddered to hear this favourite role of hers, bedevilled by such a Squalini. We were joined on coming out by Mr. Hoffman and brought him along in our carriage with us. Gave him some cold tongue to eat to take the taste of *Cenerentola* out of his mouth. He stayed some time. I like him enough, he is evidently a clever man, though he does murder the King's English—by the way— does *English*, the tongue, belong in America to the King or the President? What on earth can I say to the worthy citizens, if they ask me what I thought of the Italian opera? That it was very amusing—yes, that will do very nicely.

Sunday, October 6th

YOUNG Charles Kean called. How unfortunately plain he is! His voice is marvellously like his father's, and it pleased me to hear him speak. He was talking to my father about the various southern and western theatres, and bidding us to expect to meet strange people in those lost lands beyond the world. On one occasion, he said, when he was acting Richard the Third, some of the underlings kept their hats on while he was on stage, whereat Kean remonstrated, requesting them in a whisper to uncover, as they were in the presence of a king. To which admonition he received the following characteristic reply—"Fiddlesticks! I guess we know nothing about kings in this country!".

VI

Off to Philadelphia—Journey by boat, stage coach, and horse-drawn railway—Arrival at the Mansion House after a 10-hour journey

Monday, October 7th

ROSE (Oh horror!) at a quarter to five. Night was still brooding over the earth. Long before I was dressed the first voice I heard was that of Colonel Sibell, come to look after our luggage and see us off. At six o'clock, just as the night was folding its soft black wings, we took our departure from that mansion of little ease, the American Hotel, and our fellow lodgers, the ants, and proceeded to the Philadelphia steamboat, which started from the bottom of Barclay Street. We were recommended to the American Hotel, as the best and most comfortable in New York, and truly the charges were as high as one could have paid at the Clarendon, in the land of comfort and taxation. The rooms were a mixture of French finery and Irish dirt and disorder. The living was by no means good, the whole house being conducted on a close, scraping system of inferior accommodation and extravagant charges. On a sudden influx of visitors, sitting rooms were converted into bedrooms containing four or five beds. The number of servants was totally inadequate to the work, and the articles of common use, such as knives and spoons were so scantily provided, that when the public table was very full one day, the knives and forks for *our* dinner were obliged to be washed for theirs.

The servants, who as I said before, were just a quarter as many as the house required, had no bedrooms allocated to them, but slept anywhere, in the public rooms, or on sofas, or in drawing rooms let to private families. In short, nothing can exceed the want of order, propriety and comfort in this establishment, except the enormity of the tribute it levies upon the pilgrims and wayfarers through the land. As I said, we departed from thence, nothing loathe.

The morning was dull, dreary and damp. The steamboat was very large and commodious as all these conveyances are. I inquired of one of the passengers what the power of the engine was, and he replied he did not know exactly, but that he thought it was about forty horse power, and that, when going at speed, the engine struck thirty times a minute. This appeared to me to be a great number in so short time, but the weather shortly became wet, so I did not remain on deck to observe.

My early rising had made me very sleepy, so I came down to the third deck to sleep. These steamboats have three stories, the upper one is, as it were, a roofing or terrace on the leads of the second, a very desirable station when the weather is neither too foul nor too fair. A burning sun being, I should think, as little desirable there as a shower of rain. The second floor or deck has the advantage of the ceiling above, and yet, the sides being completely open, it is airy and allows free sight of the shores on either hand. Chairs, stools and benches are the furniture of these two decks. The one below, or third floor downwards, in fact the *ground* floor, being the one near the water, is a spacious room completely roofed and walled in, where the passengers take their meals and resort if the weather is unfavourable. At the end of this room, is a smaller cabin for the use of ladies, with beds and sofas, and all the convenience if they should be sick. There I came and slept till breakfast time.

49

Vigne's account of the pushing, thrusting, rushing, and devouring on board a western steamboat at meal times, had prepared me for rather an awful spectacle. But this I find, is by no means the case in these more civilised parts, and everything was conducted with perfect order and civility. The breakfast was good, and eaten with decency enough. Came up on the upper deck, and walked about with my father. The width of the river struck me as remarkable, but the shores were flat and uninteresting, except for the rich and varied tints of the thickets of wood, which are as superior in their brilliancy to our autumnal colouring as their gorgeous skies are to ours. Opposite the town of Amboy, the Raritan opens into a magnificent lake-like expanse round the extreme point of Staten Island.

At about half past ten, we reached the place where we leave the river, to proceed across a part of the State of New Jersey to the Delaware. The landing was beyond measure wretched. The shore shelved down to the water's edge, and its marshy, clayey, sticky soil, rendered doubly soft and squashy by the damp weather, was strewn over with broken potsherds, stones and bricks, by way of path-way. These presently failed and some slippery planks half immersed in mud were the roads to the coaches that stood ready to receive the passengers off the steamboat. Of these coaches! No Englishman can conceive the surpassing clumsiness and wretchedness of these leathern inconveniences. They are shaped something like boats, the sides being merely leathern pieces, removable at pleasure, but which, in bad weather, are buttoned down to protect the inmates from the wet. There are three seats in this machine, the middle one runs between the carriage doors, and lifts away to permit the egress and ingress of the occupants of the other seats. Into the one facing the horses Dall and I put ourselves. Presently two young ladies occupied the opposite one, a third lady and a gentleman of the same party sat in the middle seat, into which my father's huge bulk was also squeezed. Finally another man belonging to the same party ensconced himself between the two young ladies.

For the first few minutes I thought I must have fainted from the intolerable sensation of smothering which I experienced. However, the leathers being removed, and a little more air obtained, I resigned myself to my fate. Away walloped the four horses, trotting with their front and galloping with their back legs. And away we went after them, bumping, thumping, jolting, shaking, tossing and tumbling over the wickedest road, I do think, that ever wheel rumbled upon. Through bog and marsh, and ruts, wider and deeper than any Christian ruts I ever saw, with the roots of the trees protruding across our path, their boughs every now and then giving us an affectionate scratch through the windows. More than once, a half-demolished trunk or stump lying in the middle of the road, lifted us up and let us down again, with the most awful variations of our poor coach body from its natural position. Even my poor father's solid proportions could not keep their level, but were jerked up to the roof and down again every few minutes. Our companions seemed nothing dismayed by these wondrous performances, but laughed and talked at the top of their voices and with the national nasal twang. The ladies were all pretty, two of them particularly so, with their delicate fair complexions and beautiful grey eyes—but I wish that they could have held their tongues for two minutes.

The country through which we passed was woodland, flat and without variety, save what it derived from the wondrous richness and brilliancy of the autumnal foliage. Here decay indeed is beautiful, Nature appears more gloriously clad in this her fading mantle, than in all the summer's flush of bloom in our less favoured climates. I noticed several beautiful wild flowers growing among the underwood, some of which I have seen adorning with great dignity our most cultivated gardens.

The few cottages and farm-houses we passed reminded me of similar dwellings in France or Ireland, yet the peasantry here have not the same excuse for disorder and dilapidation as either the French or the Irish. The farms had the same desolate, untidy untended look, the fences carelessly put up or ill-repaired; the farming utensils sluttishly scattered about a littered yard, where the pigs seem to preside by undisputed right; house windows broken and stuffed with paper or clothes; dishevelled women and bare-footed young things. None of the stirring life and activity which such places present in England or Scotland.

After about fourteen miles we turned into swampy field, the whole fourteen coaches of us, and bag and baggage were packed into coaches which stood on the railway ready to receive us. The carriages were not drawn by steam, like those on the Liverpool railway, but by horses. Our coachful got into the first carriage of the train, thus escaping the dust which one's predecessors occasion. This vehicle had but two seats, each of which held four of us. The whole inside was lined with blazing scarlet leather, and the windows shaded with curtains of the same refreshing colour, which with the full complement of passengers, on a fine sunny American summer's day, makes a pretty a little hell as may be.

This railroad is an infinite blessing, but 'tis not yet finished, but will shortly be so, and then the whole of that horrible fourteen miles will be performed in comfort and decency in less than half the time. In about an hour and a half, we reached the end of our rail-road part of the journey, and found another steamboat waiting for us, when we all embarked on the Delaware. Again the enormous width of the river struck me with astonishment and admiration.

Such huge bodies of water mark out the country through which they run, as the future abode of the most extensive commerce and the greatest maritime power in the universe. I sat working, having finished my book, not a little discomforted by the pertinaceous staring of some of my fellow passengers. One woman in particular, after wandering round me in every direction, at last came and sat down opposite me, and literally gazed me out of countenance. One improvement they have adopted on board these boats, is to forbid smoking, except in the fore part of the vessel. I wish they would suggest that if the gentlemen would refrain from spitting about too, it would be highly aggreeable to the female part of the community. The universal practice here of this disgusting trick makes me absolutely sick. Today on board, it was a perfect shower of saliva all the time.

At about four o'clock, we reached Philadelphia, having performed the journey between that place and New York (a distance of one hundred miles) in less than ten hours, in spite of the bogs, ruts and all other impediments. The manager came to look after us and our goods, and we were stowed into a coach and conveyed to the Mansion House, the best reputed inn in Philadelphia.

VII

*A walk through Philadelphia—Charles Kemble gives a fine
performance to a full house—A comparison between Charles Kemble
and Edmund Kean—An unresponsive audience for Fazio—Fanny's
first meeting with Pierce Butler*

Tuesday, October 8th

AFTER breakfast took a walk with my father through
some of the principal streets. The town is perfect silence and solitude compared with New York, and there is
greater air of age about it too, which pleases me. The red
houses are not so fiercely red, nor the white facings so glar-
ingly white, in short, it has not so new and flaunting a look,
which is a great recommendation to me. The city is regularly built, the streets intersecting each other at right angles. We passed one or two pretty buildings in pure white
marble, and the bank in Chestnut Street, which is a beautiful little copy of the Parthenon. The shops are much better looking than those in New York. The windows are larger,
and more advantageously constructed for the display of
goods. There did not seem to be the same mixture of ven-
dibles as in the New York shops.

Came in and dressed for dinner, which was an excellent
one. The master of the house was, it seems, once a man of
independent means and a great "bon vivant". He has retained a fellow-feeling for his guests and does by them as
he would be done by.

AFTER breakfast wrote to dear Harriet. The streets were in uproar all night, people shouting and bonfires blazing, in short, electioneering fun. It seems pretty much the same the world over. Clay has it hollow here, they say. I wonder what Colonel Sibell will say to that. At twelve o'clock sallied forth with Dall to the theatre on Chestnut Street. It is very pretty, not large, but well sized and I should think favourably constructed for the voice.

After rehearsal walked about the town in quest for some coques de perles for my Bianca dress, but could not procure any. I like this town extremely. It is quieter than New York, and the shops too have a far better appearance. New York always gives me the idea of an irregular collection of temporary buildings, erected for some casual purpose, full of life and variety, but not meant to endure for any length of time. This place has a much more substantial, sober and city-like appearance.

Came home at half past two and in the hall met Mr. Staley, who is grown ten years younger since I saw him last. It always delights me to see one of our fellow passengers. But I am much disappointed at not finding Harriet Hodgkinson here. After dinner read my father some of my journal, then took coffee and went to the theatre. The house was very full, but not so full as the Park Theatre on the first night of his acting there, which accounts for the greater stillness of the audience.

I watched my father narrowly through his part tonight with great attention, and the conclusion I have come to is this; though his workmanship may be far finer than that of any other artist I ever saw, yet its very minute accuracy and refinement renders it unfit for the frame in which it is exhibited. Whoever should paint a scene calculated for so large a space as a theatre, and destined to be viewed at the distance from which an audience beholds it, with the laborious finish and fine detail of a miniature, would commit a great error of judgement. The great beauty of all my father's performances, but particularly of Hamlet, is a wonderful accuracy in the detail of the character he represents. But the result is not such as he expects, as the reward of so much labour. Few persons are able to follow such a performance with the necessary attention, and it is almost as great an exertion to *see* it understandingly as to *act* it. The amazing study of it requires a study in those who are to appreciate it, and this is far from being what the majority of spectators are either capable of or desirous of doing. I think that acting is best which skilfully husbands the actor's and spectator's powers.

At the same time, I am far from advocating that most imperfect conception and embodying of a part which Kean allows himself—acting detached passages alone and leaving all the others, and the entire character indeed, utterly destitute of unity, or the semblance of any consistency whatsoever. Kean and my father are each other's antipodes, and in adopting their different styles of acting, it is evident that each has been guided as much by his own physical and intellectual individuality as by any fixed principles of art. The one, Kean, possesses particular physical characteristics—an eye like an orb of light, a voice, exquisitely touching and melodious in its tenderness, and in the harsh dissonance of passion, terribly true. To these he adds the intellectual ones of vigour, intensity, amazing power of concentrating effort. These give him an entire mastery over his audience in all striking, sudden and impassioned passages.

My father possesses certain physical defects—a faintness

of colouring in the face and eye, a weakness of voice. And the corresponding intellectual deficiencies, a want of intensity, vigour and concentrating power. These circumstances have led him to give his attention to the finer and more fleeting shades of character, the more graceful and delicate manifestations of feeling, the exquisite variety of minor parts, the classic keeping of a highly wrought note. Polished and refined tastes, an acute sense of the beauty of harmonious proportions, and a native grace, gentleness and refinement of mind and manner, have been his prompters. But they cannot inspire those startling and tremendous bursts of passion which belong to the highest walks of tragedy, and to which he never gave their fullest expression. I fancy my aunt Siddons united the excellencies of both these styles. But to return to my father's Hamlet—every time I see it, something strikes me afresh in the detail. Nothing to my mind can exceed the exquisite beauty of his last—"Go on, I follow thee", to the Ghost. There is one thing in which I do not believe my father ever has been or ever will be excelled—his high and noble bearing, his gallant, graceful, courteous deportment, his perfect good-breeding on the stage.

Thursday, October 10th

ROSE rather late, wrote journal and then went to rehearsal. After rehearsal came home, habited, and went to the riding-school to try some horses. Merci de moi! what quadrupeds! How they did wallop and shamble about, poor half-broken dumb brutes! they knew no better. The natives here are quite satisfied with their shuffling, rollicking, mongrel paces, half trot, half canter, so it is not worth while to break horses in a Christian-like fashion for them. I found something that I think my father can ride with tolerable comfort, but I must go again tomorrow and see after something for myself.

Friday, October 11th

AFTER breakfast sat writing journal and a letter to Harriet. After rehearsal walked down to the riding school with my father, but the horse I was to look at had not arrived, but my father saw the grey. We were there for some time, and during that time, a tall, thin, unhappy-looking gentleman, who had gotten up on some great hulking raw-boned horse, kept trotting round and round, with his legs dangling down, sans stirrups, at the rate of a mile and a quarter an hour, occasionally ejaculating in the mildest of tones—"keome up! keome up!", whereat the lively brute proceeded at the very same rate, at the very same pace, and this went on till I wondered at the man and beast.

Came home, put things out for the theatre and went there at six. The house was very full, and Dall and my father said I was extremely ungracious in my acknowledgement of their greeting. I cannot tell, I did not mean to be so. I made them three courtesies, and what could woman do more. Of course, I can neither feel or look so glad to see them as I am to see my own dear London people, neither can I be as profound in my obeisance as when my audience is civil enough to rise to me.

My Fazio had a pair of false whiskers on, which distilled a black stripe of trickling cement down his cheeks, and kept me in agony every time he had to embrace me. This audience is the most unapplausive I ever acted to. They were very attentive certainly, but how they did make me work! 'Tis amazing how much an audience loses by this hanging back, even when the silence proceeds from an unwillingness to interrupt a good performance. In reality it is the greatest compliment an actor can receive, yet he is deprived by that very stillness of half his power. Excitement is reciprocal between performer and audience. In that last scene in *Fazio*, half the effect I produce is derived from the applause I receive, the very noise and tumult of which tends to heighten the nervous energy which the scene begets. I know that my aunt Siddons frequently said the same thing.

Saturday, October 12th

AFTER breakfast wrote journal and put on my habit, which I had no sooner done than the perverse clouds began to rain. The horses came at two, but the weather was so bad I sent them away again. After dinner came to my room and tried to scribble something for the *Mirror*, at my father's request, the editors having made a special entreaty to him that I might write something for them. I could not accomplish anything, and they must take something I have by me.

Came down and found a young gentleman sitting with my father—one Mr. Butler. He was a pretty-spoken youth enough. He drank tea with us and offered to ride with me. He has, it seems, a great fortune, consequently I suppose, in spite of his lack of inches, is a great man.

VIII

Charles Kemble's Romeo—Position of American women in society—
Riding along the Schuylkill—Full house for The Hunchback—Visit
to the Pennsylvania

Sunday, October 14th

AT three o'clock Dall and I sallied forth to church. Following the silver voices of the Sabbath bells, we entered a church with a fine simple facade and found ourselves in the midst of a Presbyterian congregation. 'Tis now
upwards of eight years since, as a schoolgirl, I used to at-
tent a dissenters' chapel. The form of worship, though displeasing to me in itself, borrowed a charm today from old
association. How much of the past did it recall! After dinner, a gentleman of the press by name Willis Taylor Clarke,
paid us an evening visit. He seems an intelligent enough
young man. When he spoke of the autumnal woods by the
Oneida lake, his expressions were poetical and enthusiastic
and he pleased me. When had gone wrote another letter to
Harriet and went to bed.

Monday, October 15th

WENT to rehearsal, the day was cold but beautifully
bright and clear. The pure, fresh, invigorating air
and gay sunlight together with the delightfully clean streets,
and the pretty mixture of trees and buildings in this nice
town, caused me to rejoice as I walked along. So—we are

to act *The Gamester* here. Went and ordered a dress for that play, my own being in New York. At six went to the theatre. I never beheld anything more gorgeous than the sky at sunset. Autumn is an emperor here, clothed in crimson and gold and canopied with ruddy glowing skies.

The play was *Romeo and Juliet*. My father was the "youngest of that name" for want of a better, or rather, of a worse. How beautiful this performance must have been when the youthful form made that appear natural, which now seems the triumph of art over nature. Garrick said, that to act Romeo required a grey hand upon green shoulders. Indeed, 'tis difficult! It is difficult to act with my father. One's imagination need toil but little to see in him the thing he represents. With all other Romeos, though they were much younger men, I have had to do double work; first to get rid of the material obstacle staring me in the face, and then to substitute some more congenial representative of that sweetest vision of youth and love.

The audience here are, without exception, the most disagreeable I ever played to. Not a single hand did they give the balcony scene, or my father's scene with the Friar. They applauded vehemently at the end of my draught scene and a great deal at the end of the play, but they are intolerably dull and it is all but impossible to act to them. The man who acted Capulet did it better than any Capulet I ever acted with. The Nurse, besides looking admirable, acted her part very well, and 'tis hard to please me after poor dear Mrs. Davenport. The house was literally crammed from floor to ceiling. Came home hoarse, though my voice was a good deal better today.

A T two o'clock rode out with my father. The day was most enchanting, mild, bright and sunny, but the roads were deplorable and the country utterly dull. My horse was a hard-mouthed, half-broken beast, a perfect rack on hoofs, how it did jog and jumble me! However my bones are young and my courage good and I don't mind a little hard work. But the road was so villanously bad and the surrounding country so weary, dull, stale and unprofitable, that I was heartily sick of my ride. But presently the river, bright and broad and placid as a lake, with its beautiful banks and rainbow-coloured woods, opened upon us. We crossed a covered wooden bridge, and followed the water's edge. The rich colours of the foliage cast a warm light over the transparent face of the mirror-like stream, and far along the winding shore, a mingled mantel of gorgeous tints lay over the woody banks, and was reflected in the still sunny river. Indeed it was lovely! but our time was growing short, and we had to turn home, which we did by a pleasant and more direct path.

My riding cap seemed to excite universal marvel wherever we passed. We came in at five o'clock, dressed and dined. Just as I finished dinner, a most beautiful, fragrant and delicious nosegay was brought to me, with a very laconic note from a Philadelphia "friend", dashed under, as though from a Quaker. Whoever 'tis from, hath my most unbounded gratitude. Spent an ecstatic half hour arranging my flowers in glasses, and while doing so, a card was brought up. Presently Mr. Bell came in, another of our *Pacific* fellow-sailors. It pleases me to see them as they seem to bring us nearer to England. He gave us a dreadful account of his arrival in Baltimore, and of the state to which the cholera had reduced that city. Mr. Staley amused me by telling me that he had heard my behaviour canvassed with censure by some man or other, who had met me at Mr. Hone's, and who was horrified at my taking up a book and then a newspaper, and, in short, in being neither magical nor comical at a dinner party. Of course, I must seem a very strange animal to them, but they seem just as strange to me.

Wednesday, October 17th

AT eleven went to rehearsal. It seems there has been fighting and rushing and tearing of coats at the box-office, and one man has made forty dollars, by purchasing and reselling tickets at an increased price. After rehearsal, came home and Mr. Bell called and sat for some time. He sails for England on the twenty fourth. His description of American life and manners (and he knows both, for he has lived constantly in this country) is anything but agreeable.

The dignified and graceful influence which married women, among us, exercise over the tone of manners, uniting the duties of home with the charms of social life, is utterly unknown here. Married women are either house-drudges and nursery-maids, or, if they appear in society, comparative cyphers. The retiring, modest, youthful bearing which among us distinguishes girls of fifteen or sixteen is equally unknown. Society is entirely led by chits, who in England would be sitting behind a pinafore. The consequence is, that it has neither the elegance, refinement nor the propriety which belongs to ours, but is a noisy, racketty, vulgar congregation of flirting boys and girls, alike without style or decorum.

When Mr. Bell had gone, practised for half an hour till it was time to go to the theatre. The house was crammed again and the play better acted than I have ever seen it out of London; though Mrs. Candour had stuck upon her head a bunch of feathers which threatened the gods. Lady Sneerwell had dragged all her hair off her face, which needed to be as pretty as it was to endure such exposure. I do not wonder that the New Yorkers did not approve of my Lady Teasle. If, as Henry Berkley says, Mrs. Charles Augustus Davis of New York is their idea of the perfection of good breeding, well may my delineation of a lady be condemned as "nothing particular". Yet I am sorry that I must continue to lie under their censure, for I, unfortunately for myself, have seen *real* ladies, who, from all I can see, hear and understand, differ widely from the good manners of their "beau ideal". The fact is, I am not *genteel* enough, and I am conscious of it. The play went off remarkably well.

Thursday, October 18th

HERE is the end of October, the very mourning time of the year with us, and my room is full of flowers, and the sun is so bright and powerful, that it is impossible to go out with a shawl or without a parasol. At half past two rode out with my father. We took the road to the Schuykill at once, through Arch Street, which is a fine, broad, long street, running parallel with Chestnut Street. Turning between some rising banks, through a defile where the road wound up a hill, we caught a glimpse of a white house standing on the sunny slope of a green rise. The undulating grounds around were all bathed in a warm light, relieved only by the massy shadows of the thick woods that sheltered them. It was a bit of England. Some good farming and tidy out-houses completed the resemblance, and made me think that this must be the dwelling of some of my country-men. How can they live here? here, even in the midst of what is fair and peaceful in nature, I think my home would haunt me, and the far-off chiming of the waves against her white shores resound in my ears through the smooth flowing of the Schuylkill. After pursuing a level uninteresting road for some time, we turned off to the right, and had a most enchanting glimpse of the river and its woody shores. The river makes a bend just above the water-works, and the curving banks form a lovely little sunny bay. It was more like a lake here, than a flowing stream. The bright hues of the heavens and the glowing tints of the wooded shores were mirrored with wondrous vividness of its bosom. I never saw such gorgeousness or such perfect harmony of colour. The eye was drunk with beauty, and I, who am not a painter, was half crazy that I was not. We rode on through scenery of the same description, passing on our way a farm and dairy, where the cattle were standing, not in open pasture-land, but in the corner of forest ground, all bright with the golden shedding of the trees. It was very picturesque.

Returned home about half past five and found another beautiful nosegay waiting for me, from my unknown furnisher of sweets. This is almost as tantalising as it is civil— I would give half my lovely flowes to find out who sends them. Distributed them all over the room and was as happy as a queen. Mr. Clarke called, and as my father had to go out on business, Dall and I were obliged to entertain that worthy youth. He seems to have a wonderful veneration for a parcel of scribblers whose names were never heard of in England, beyond the limits of their own narrow coteries. But he speaks like an enthusiast of the woods and waters of his glorious country, and I excuse his taste in poetry. Isn't this strange! that a man who can feel the amazing might, majesty and loveliness of nature, can endure for a moment the mawkish scribbling of these poetasters.

Tuesday, October 23rd

A T ten o'clock went to rehearsal for *The Hunchback* and then *Fazio*—this is tolerably hard work, with acting every night. We don't steal our money, that's one comfort. Came home and went on with my letter to Harriet. While doing so, was interrupted by the entrance of a strange woman, who sat herself down, apparently in much confusion. She told me a story of great distress, and claimed my assistance as a fellow-countrywoman. I had not a farthing of money, Dall and my father were out, so I took the reference she gave me and promised to inquire into her condition. The greatest evil arising from the many claims of this sort which are made upon us wherever we go, is the feeling of distrust and suspicion which they engender. "Oh, ten to one, an imposter", is soon said, and instances enough may be found to prove the probability of such a conclusion. Yet in this sweeping condemnation one real case of misery may be included, and that possibility must make us pause.

Wednesday, October 24th

A T half past one, went with Dall to find out something about my yesterday's poor woman. The references were satisfactory, that is, they proved that she was poor and in distress, and willing to work. I gave her what I could, and the man by whom she is employed seems anxious to afford her work, so I hope she will get on a little. Came home, finished a letter to Harriet and went to the theatre. It seems there have been,

"Bloody noses and cracked crowns,
And all the currents of a heady fight",

at the box office, and truly the house bore witness thereto, for it was crammed from floor to ceiling. The play was *The Hunchback*. I played very well, in spite of no green carpet, and no letter in the letter scene, which lost one of my favourite points—one that I am fond of, because it is all my own.

Friday, October 26th

WHILE I was dressing Dall, like a good angel, came in with three letters from England in her hand. The love of excellent friends is one of God's greatest blessings and deserves our utmost thankfulness. A Mr., Mrs., and young Mr. Biddle called upon us. They are the only inhabitants of this good city who have done us that honour.

As soon as my father came in, we sallied forth to see the giantess of a ship the Americans have been building. I hooked myself up to Mr. Staley and away we strode, Dall and my father struggling after us. The day was most beautiful, bright, sunny and fresh. After walking at an immense pace for some time, we bethought us of looking for our "poursuivants", but neither sign nor vestige of them appeared. We stood still and waited, and went on, and stood still again. At length we wisely agreed that they had probably made their way to the navy yard, and thither we proceeded. We found them waiting for us, and entered the building where this lady of the seas was propped upon a hundred stays, surrounded with scaffolding, with galleries running round from the floor to the ceiling. We went on deck, in fact, the *Pennsylvania* has been boarded by the English in our persons, before she sets foot on the sea. How I should like to see that ship launched, how she will sweep down from her holdings and settle to the water as a swan before swimming out.

My father and Mr. Staley indulged in sundry right English bits of bragging as they stood at her stern, looking down the enormous deck. I wish I knew her exact measurements. She is the largest ship ever built, larger than any East Indiaman, the largest ship in the world. How the sea will groan under her!

Came home just in time to dine, at six, went to the theatre, play, *The Hunchback.* I played so-so, the audience are detestable. The majority are so silent that they not only do not applaud the acting, but forbear to notice all noises in the house, in consequence of which some impudent women amused themselves with talking during the whole play, much louder than the players. At one time their impertinent racket so bewildered me, that I was all but out, and this without the audience once interfering to silence them. Perhaps, however, that would have been an unwarrantable interference with the liberties of the people. I indulged them with a very significant glance, and at one moment was sorely tempted to request them to hold their tongues.

IX

Saturday, October 27th

THE poor sick lady whose pretty children I meet running about the stairs, sent to say she would be very
glad if I would go in and see her. I had had sundry inward
promptings to this effect before, but was withheld by the
real English dread of intruding. At eleven went to rehearsal
and on my return, called on Mrs. Dulaney. She interested
me most extremely, I would have stayed longer with her,
but feared she might exhaust herself by the exertion of conversing. On my return to my room, I sent her Mr. Clarke's
annuals, and the volume of Mrs. Heman's poetry he lent
me. Began practising, when in walked that interesting youth,
Mr. Edward Biddle, with a nosegay as big as himself in his
hand. Flowers, sweet, blooming fresh, delicious flowers in
the last days of October, the very sackcloth season of the
year. How they do rejoice my spirit. He sat some time,
making excessively fine speeches to me. While he was here,
arrived another bouquet from my unknown friend. When
my visitor was gone, wrote to Harriet till dinner time. After dinner spent nearly the whole afternoon in dressing my
pretty flowers. I sent some of them in to poor Mrs. Dulaney.

I finished my letter to Harriet, then went to the theatre.

69

It was my benefit—*The Provoked Husband.* The house was very good. I played so-so, and looked very nice. What fine breeding this play is to be sure. It is quite refreshing to act it, but it must be heathen Greek to the American *exclusives,* I should think.

H AD time only to swallow a mouthful of breakfast and off to church. I must say it requires a great deal of fortitude to go into an American church. There are no pew openers, and the people appear to rush indifferently into any seats that are vacant. We went into a pew where there were two women and a man, who did not take up one half of it, but who, nevertheless looked most ungracious at our coming into it. They did not move to make way or accomodate us, but remained with very discourteous sulkiness spread over twice as much space as they required. The spirit of independence seems to preside even in the house of God. This congregation, by frequenting an Episcopalian temple, evidently professed the form of faith of the English church. Yet they neither uttered the responses, nor observed any of the directions in the Common Prayer Book. Thus, during portions of the worship where kneeling is enjoined, they sat or stood, and while the Creed was being read, half the congregation were reclining comfortably in their pews. The same thing with the psalms, and all parts of the service. The whole experience of the congregation was that of indifference, indolence and irreverence, and was highly displeasing to my eye.

Throughout all the northern states, and particularly those of New England, the Unitarian form of faith prevails. It appears to me to be admirably suited to the spiritual necessities of this portion of the Americans. They are a reasoning,

not an imaginative race, and it therefore suits their character to have a religious creed divested of mysteries and of
long and laborious ceremonies, which too often engross the
time without the attention of the worshipper. They are poor
too, comparatively speaking, and were they so inclined,
could little afford either the splendid pageantry which the
Romish priesthood requires or the less glaring, but not less
expensive revenues which the Episcopalian clergy enjoy.
Their form of religion is a simple one, a short one and a
cheap one. It appears to me to be as much fitted for this
people, as the marvellous legends and magnificent shows of
the Romish church were to the early European nations. The
church in America is not, as with us, a mere means of living. There are no rich benefices or over-swelled bishop-
ricks to be hoped for. The pecuniary remuneration of the
clergy depends upon the generosity of the congregations.

Thursday, October 30th

AT eleven went to rehearsal, then came home and practised for some time. All of a sudden the door opened
and in walked Colonel Sibell with my father—he had just
arrived from New York. He dined with us, and after dinner, went to the theatre. The house was very good, the play,
Much Ado About Nothing. I played well, but what an audience it is. I have often been recommended, in cases of
nervousness on the stage, to consider the audience as just
so many cabbages, and indeed a small stretch of fancy would
enable me to do so here. Received an invitation to dinner
from the Biddles. "One exception makes a rule", say the
scholars, and by that same token the Philadelphians are
about the most inhospitable set of people it has ever been
my good fortune to fall with. I am sure there is no town in
Europe where my father could fix his residence for a week,

without being immediately found out by most of the residents of any literary acquirements or knowledge relating to art. I am sure that neither in France, Italy or Germany could he take up his abode in any city, without immediately being sought by those most worth knowing in it. I confess it surprised me, therefore, when I found that during a month's residence in Philadelphia, scarcely a creature came near us, and but one house was hospitably opened to us. Everywhere else in America, our reception was very different, and I can only attribute the want of courtesy we met with in Philadelphia, to the greater prevalence of that very small spirit of dignity which is always afraid of committing itself.

Friday, November 2nd

A BRIGHT sunny day, too hot for a fire, windows open, shutters closed, and the room full of flowers. How the sweet summer time stays lingering here. Found Colonel Sibell in the drawing room. Mr. Pierce Butler called, he stayed but a short time and went out with Colonel Sibell. Mrs. Dulaney came in and sat with me. She played to me and sang—"Should those fond hopes ever leave thee". Her voice was as thin as her pale transparent hands. She appeared to me much better than when I last saw her, but she presently told me that she had just been swallowing eighty drops of laudanum, poor thing!

When she was gone, went with my father and Dall to call on old Mrs. Adamson. The day was so hot I could hardly endure my boa. The election was going on, the streets full of rabblement, the air full of huzzaing and the sky obscured with star-spangled banners. We went round the Town House, and looked at the window out of which Jefferson read the Act of Independence, that proclaimed the separation between England and America. In beholding this fine young giant of a world, with all its magnificent capacities for greatness, I think every Englishman must feel regret at the unjust and unwise course of policy which alienated such a child from the parent government. But far from regretting that America has thrown off her allegiance, and regarding her as a rebellious subject, and irreverent child, England will surely, ere long, learn to look upon this country as the inheritor of her glory, the younger England, destined to perpetuate the language, the memory, the virtues of the noble land from which she is descended.

After dinner, received another beautiful nosegay. At six went to the theatre. The sunset was glorious, the rising of the moon most beautiful. We were obliged to go all manner of roundabout to the play-house in order to avoid the rabble that choked up the principal streets. I, by way of striking salutary awe into the hearts of all rioters who might come across our path, brandished my father's sword out of the coach window the whole way along. The play was *Venice Preserved,* my father playing Jaffier. I played pretty well, the house was very good, but at the end I was really half dead.

On our return home, met a procession of electioneers carrying triangular paper lanterns upon poles, with political "sentiments" scribbled thereon, which, however, I could not distinguish. I found another most exquisite nosegay waiting for me at home, so fragrant and fresh. Colonel Sibell came in after supper, and wondered that I had played better to my father's Jaffier than to Mr. Keppel's. Heaven bless the world, for a conglomerated amalgamation of fools!

Monday, November 5th

GUY Fawlke's day, and no squibs, no firing of pistols, no bonfires, nor parading about of ferocious-looking straw men. Ah! these poor people never had a king and two Houses of Parliament, and don't know what a mercy it is they were not blown up before they passed the Reform Bill.

Rose at half past five and dressed myself by candlelight. Mrs. Dulaney sent in to ask me if I would see her but I had no time, so sent her a note. Started from the Mansion House (which is a very nice inn, kept by the civilest of people) and reached the quay just in time to see the first rosy breaking of the clouds over the Delaware. I am sorry to leave Philadelphia. I like the town, and the little I have seen of the inhabitants, very much—I mean in private, for they are intolerable audiences. There is an air of stability, of well to do, and occasionally of age in the town that reminds me of England. Then, as far as my yesterday's dinner will allow me to judge, I should say that not only the style of living, but the society was superior to that which I saw in New York.

The morning, in spite of all Mr. Staley's prophecies, was beautiful beyond description. The river was like the smoothest glass. The sky was bright and cloudless, and the tints of the woods were what no words can convey the slightest idea of. The whole land at a distance appeared to lie under an atmosphere of glowing colour, richer than any crimson mantle that ever clothed the emperors of the olden world, and all this, illuminated by a sun which we would have thought too hot for June. It was very beautiful. I did not, however, see much of it, for I was overcome with fatigue and slept both in the steamboat and in the stage coach. When we embarked on the Raritan, I had intended lying down in the cabin, but the jolting of those bitter roads had made every woman sick and the cabin was horrible beyond description.

Came up on deck, and worked till within a quarter of a mile of New York, when I went on the upper deck and walked about with Colonel Sibell. I asked Captain Seymour how often the engine would strike in a minute, and he told me thirty-six times. We had a race coming down the Raritan with the Union steamboat. The *Water Witch* beat her hollow, but she came so near as to make our water rough, and so impede our progress.

The sun went down in a gloomy sky, though the day had been so fine. Our second landing at New York was rather melancholy—shall I ever forget the first! Came to our comfortless American Hotel, dressed and dined.

Tuesday, November 6th New York

AFTER dinner Colonel Sibell called, and very nearly caused a blow up between me and my father. He came preaching to me the necessity of restoring those lines of Bianca's in the judgement scene, which were originally omitted, afterwards restored by me at Milman's request, and again cut off, on finding that they only lengthened the scene, without producing the slightest effect. My father appeared perfectly to agree with me, but added that I might as well oblige the people. I said I would do no such thing. People sitting before the curtain must not come and tell me what I am to do behind it. Not one of a hundred in the first place, understand what they are talking about. Why therefore, am I to alter my work at their suggestion, when each particular scene has cost me more consideration than they ever bestowed upon any whole play in their lives. So, all things considered the good New Yorkers must be contented with the judgement of Miss O'Neill, my father and their obedient humble servant.

Wednesday, November 7th

OUR breakfast was so bad none of us could eat anything. At half past one went with my father to walk
on the Battery, while Colonel Sibell and Dall went to see
if we could get any decent lodgings and wholesome eatables. The day was melancholy, grey and cold, with a full
fresh wind rattling the leaves along. The Jersey shore and
Staten Island with their withered woods all clothed in their
dark autumnal hues, at a distance reminded me of the
heathery hills of Scotland.

Dall and the Colonel joined us and we walked up Broadway together. Darkness, dinginess and narrowness were the
attributes of the apartments into which we were shown.
Then, as the Colonel had never eaten in the house, he did
not know what our food might be. *Resolved*—that we were
better off where we are, and so returned to the American.
Mr. Wallack called to go with my father to Mrs. Wallack's,
where they are to dine. He certainly is one of the hand-
somest of men I ever saw, but he looks half dead and is
working himself to death, it seems. He told me that Boston
was the most charming town in America.

Thursday, November 8th

AT the end of dinner, Colonel Sibell called, and he read
us a paragraph in one of the Philadelphia papers about
me, and all my good parts. There was actually a column of
them. It was well written, for I was absolute perfection. Except, in one respect, the hauteur and disdain with which I
had treated the "rank and fashion of Philadelphia". Now
this was not true, for, so to speak candidly, I did not know
that there were such things as rank and fashion in all
America. However, the article made me laugh extremely,

for, as I could not help observing, "there are *real* lords and ladies in my country". I think the pretension to pre-eminence in the various societies of North America, is founded upon these grounds. In Boston, a greater degree of mental cultivation; in New York, the possession of wealth; and a lady, of whom I inquired the other day, what constituted the superiority of the aristocracy in Philadelphia, replied, "Why, birth, to be sure".

Saturday, November 10th

AT six o'clock Dall roused me and grumpily enough I arose. Soon Colonel Sibell came, and we set off to walk to the quay. Just as we were nearing Barclay Street, the bell rang from the steamboat, to summon all loiterers on board and forthwith we rushed. We got on board in plenty of time, but Dall was nearly killed with the pace at which we had walked. One of the first persons we saw was Mr. Pendleton Hosack, who was going up to his father's place beyond West Point, by name Hyde Park, which sounds mighty magnificent. I soon ascended to the first deck with Colonel Sibell and we paced to and fro till breakfast time. The morning was gray and sad looking, and I feared we should not have a fine day. However, soon the clouds parted, and the blue serene eyes of heaven looked down upon the waters, the waves began to sparkle, though the sun had not yet appeared. At eight o'clock we went down to breakfast. Nobody who had not seen it, can conceive the strange aspect of the long room of one of these fine boats at mealtime. The crowd, the hurry, the confusion of tongues, the enormous consumption of eatables, the mingled demands for more, the cloud of black waiters hovering down the sides of the immense tables, the hungry eager faces seated at them, form altogether a most amusing subject of contemplation.

As far as regards the speed, safety and convenience with which these vessels enable one to perform what would be in any other conveyance most fatiguing journeys, they are admirable inventions. Nothing can exceed the comfort with which they are fitted up, the skill with which they are managed, and the alacrity with which passengers are taken up from or landed at the various points along the river. The steamer goes at the rate of fifteen miles an hour, and in less than two minutes when approaching any place of landing, the engine stops, the boat is lowered, and away darts the tiny skiff, held by a rope to the main boat. As soon as it grazes the land, its freight, animate and inanimate, is bundled out, the boat hauls itself back in an instant, and immediately the machine is in motion, and the vessel bounding over the water like a race horse.

To an English person, the mere circumstance of being the whole day in a crowd, is a nuisance. As to privacy at any time, or under any circumstances 'tis a thing that enters not into the imagination of an American. They do not seem to comprehend that to be from sunrise to sunset one hundred and fifty people confined in a steamboat, is in itself a great misery, or that to be left by oneself, can ever be desirable. They live all the days of their lives in a throng, eat at ordinaries of two or three hundred, sleep five or six in a room, take pleasure in droves and travel in swarms. It is perfectly intolerable to me. But then I have more than even the national English abhorrence of coming into contact with strangers. There is no moment of my life when I would not rather be alone, than in company, feeling, as I often do, the society of even those I love a burthen. I think this constant living in public is one reason why the young women here are much less shy and retiring than English girls. Instead of the domestic privacy in which women among us are accustomed to live and move, here they are inces-

santly, as Mr. Bancroft says, "en evidence". An English girl
of sixteen, put on board one of these Noah's arks, would
look and feel like a scared thing.

To return to our progress. After losing sight of New York,
the river becomes narrower in its bed, and the banks on
either side assume a higher and more rocky appearance. A
fine range of basaltic rock, called the Palisadoes, rising to
a height of some hundred feet from the water on the left,
forms a natural rampart overhanging the river for several
miles. While despatching breakfast, the reflection of the sun's
rays on the water flickered to and fro upon the cabin ceiling, through the windows we saw the bright foam round
the paddles sparkling like frothed gold in the morning light.
I walked on deck without my bonnet, enjoying the delicious wind that was as bracing as a shower-bath. Mr.
Pendleton most civilly offered me, when I returned to New
York, the use of a horse, and himself as escort to a beautiful
ride beyond Hoboken, which offer was very gratefully received by me.

As we passed the various parts of the river, each of my
three companions drew my attention to them, and so I had
three variations of the same anecdote at each point of ob-
servation. On we boiled past Spiteendevil creek, where the
waters of the broad Hudson join with those of the East River,
and circle with their arms the island of Manhattan. Past
the last stupendous reach of the Palisadoes, which seems to
grow with the mariner's onward progress, and bears witness
to the justice with which Hudson, on his exploring voyage
up the river, christened it, the "weary point".

We passed the light-house of Stoney Point, now the
peaceful occupant of the territory where the blood of English
veins was poured out by English hands, during the struggle
between old established tyranny and the infant liberties of
this giant world.

At about a quarter to eleven the buildings of West Point were seen, perched upon the rock side, overhanging the water. Above was the woody rise upon whose summit stands the large hotel, the favourite resort of visitors during the summer season. We left the boat, or rather she left us, and presently we saw her holding her course far up the bright water and between the hills, where lay the bright little town of Newburgh, its white buildings glittering in the sunshine.

We toiled up the ascent and over the unshaded downs that form the parade ground for the cadets. West Point is a military establishment containing some two hundred and fifty pupils, who are here educated for the army under the superintendence of experienced officers. The buildings in which they reside and pursue their various studies, stand upon a grassy knoll on the top of the rocky bank of the river, and commanding a most enchanting view of its course. They are not particularly extensive, but commodious and well-ordered. I am told they have a good library, but on reaching the dwelling of Mr. Cozzens (proprietor of the hotel, which being shut, he received us most courteously at his own house), I felt so weary that I thought it impossible I should stir again for the whole day, so declined seeing it.

Finding it wanted a full hour till dinner time, it was agreed that we should go up to the fort, and we set off under the guidance of one of Mr. Cozzens' servants, who had orders not to go too fast with us. I had thought that I was tired and could not stir, even to follow the leisurely steps of our cicerone, but tangled brake and woodland path soon aroused my curiosity, and I presently outstripped our party, guide and all, and began pursuing my upward path. Alone, alone, I was alone and happy, and went on my way rejoicing, climbing and climbing still, till the green mound of thick turf and the ruined rampart of the fort arrested my progress. I coasted the broken wall, I looked down, and for a moment my breath seemed to stop—I was filled with awe. The beauty and wild sublimity of what I beheld seemed almost to crush my faculties—I felt dizzy as if my senses were drowning—I felt as though I had been carried into the immediate presence of God. Though I were to live a thousand years I never can forget it. I stood filled with amazement and delight, till the footsteps of my companions roused me, but I peremptorily forbade his doing so, and was clambering on alone, when the voice of our guide assured me that the path I was pursuing was impassable, and I arrested my course. My father beckoned to me from above not to pursue my track, so running round the wall I joined my father on his high stand, where he was holding his arms to me.

For two or three minutes we mingled exclamations of delight and surprise, and he then led me to the brink of the rampart, and looking down I beheld the path I was then following suddenly break off on the edge of a precipice several hundred feet down in the valley. It made me gulp to look at it.

We came down from the mountain at about half past one, our party having been joined by the Governor of the College, who very courteously came toiling up to Fort Putnam to pay his compliments to us. Mr. Cozzens very considerately gave us our dinner in a private room, instead of seating us with all the West Point officers. He himself is a very intelligent courteous person, and during the short time we were his guests, showed us every possible attention and civility. We had scarce finished our dinner, when in rushed a waiter to tell us that the boat was now in sight. Away we trotted anyhow fashion, down the hill. The steamer came puffing up the gorge between the mountains and in a moment, we were bundled into the boat, hauled alongside and landed on the deck, and the glorious highlands all a-glowing in the rosy sunset, began to recede from us. Just as we were put-

ting off from shore, a tiny skiff turned the base of the opposite hill, evidently making to the point whence we embarked. I have since learned that it contained a messenger
to us, from a gentleman bearing our name, and distantly
connected with us, proprietor of some large iron works on
the shore opposite West Point. However, our kinsman was
too late, and we were already losing sight of West Point
when his boat reached the shore.

Our progress homeward was if anything more enchanting than our coming out had been. The sun went down in
splendour, leaving the world robed in glorious beauty. As
the day fell, the volumes of smoke from our steamboat
chimneys, became streams of fiery sparks, which glittered
over the water with a strange unearthly effect. I sat on deck
watching the world grow dark, till my father, afraid of the
night air, bade me go down. And there, in spite of the
chattering of a score of women and the squalling of as many
children, I slept profoundly till we reached New York.

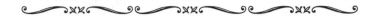

X

Riding with the Hosacks—Another expedition on horseback—A party at the Hones—"English jealousy"?—Another party at the Hones—A military parade in New York

Saturday, November 17th, 1832

THE Hosacks called for me in the carriage at eleven and then we mounted our steeds in Warren Street to escape the crowd in Broadway. We rode down to the ferry. The creature on top of which I sat was a real butcher's horse. However, it did not shake me or pull my arms much, so I was content. As to a horse properly broken, I have done looking for it in this land.

We went into the steamboat on our horses. The mist lay thick on the river and the wind blew bitterly keen and cold. Our riding party was Mr. Pendleton Hosack, who I like, Mrs. Hosack, whom I like also, in spite of her outlandish riding habit. After landing, we set off at a brisk canter to Weehawk. None of these people know how to ride. They just go at whatever pace their horse likes, sitting as back as they can in the saddle, and tugging hard at the reins, to the infinite detriment of their own hands and their horses' mouths.

When we reached the height, we dismounted and walked through the woods that crown the cliffs, which here rise to an elevation of some hundred feet above the river. Our walk terminated at a little rocky promontory, called the Devil's Pulpit, where, as legends say, Satan was wont to preach loud enough to drown the sound of Sabbath bells in New York. The Hudson far below, lay leaden and sullen, the woods along the shores looked withered and wintery, and the effect of the whole was very sad and beautiful.

We mounted our horses again, and Mrs. Hosack complained that her's pulled her wrists dreadfully, so I exchanged steed with her. The lady proprietress of the grounds over which we had been walking and riding, invited us into her house, but being mounted, I declined and we set off for the pavilion. Just as we arrived there it began to rain. Mercy on me and Mrs. Hosack! how our arms will ache tomorrow! this worthy animal of hers had a mouth a little worse than a donkey's. Arrived at the pavilion, we dismounted and swallowed sundry champagnes and lumps of plum cake, which were singularly refreshing. We set off again and presently it began to pelt with rain. We reached and crossed the ferry without getting very wet. Arranged to ride on Wednesday, if fine, and so home. Upon the whole, rather satisfied with expedition.

Sunday, November 18th

THE muscles of my arms (for I have such unladylike things) stand out like lumps of stone, with all the fine exercise they had yesterday. I wonder how Mrs. Hosack's shoulders and arms feel?

Monday, November 19th

AFTER dinner pottered about till time to got to the theatre. The house was very good. My benefit—the play, *Much Ado About Nothing.* I played very well, I am so much improved in my comedy acting. Came home in a coach— it poured with rain. The accounts of cholera in New Orleans are frightful—they have the yellow fever there too. Poor people! what an awful visitation!

Tuesday, November 20th

A T twelve went and called on Mrs. Hosack. The day was bright but bitter cold, with a keen piercing wind that cuts one in half, but it was delicious. We were brought into a room where there was a fire fit to roast an ox. No wonder the women here are delicate and subject to cold, and die of consumption. Here these were sitting absolutely in an oven, in clothes fit only for the hottest days in summer, instead of wrapping themselves up well and trotting out, and warming their blood wholesomely with good hard exercise. Settled to ride tomorrow if fine. Came home and found Howard Payne and Mr. Bayard with my father. What a very bad expression of face the former has—sneering and false, terrible! I looked at Mr. Bayard with much respect. He was a pale, sickly-looking man, without anything at all remarkable in the expression of his countenance. While they were here Mr. Hosack called to settle about tomorrow. He is a nice person, sensible and civil, and civil in the right way. Arrangements were made for dear Dall's going, which I rejoiced in greatly, as I do not like leaving her behind.

At half past five went to the theatre. House very good—play, *The Hunchback*. I played so-soish. Van Buren was at the play, and at the end somebody in the house exclaimed—"Three cheers for Van Buren!", whereupon a mingled chorus of applause and hisses arose. The Vice President looked rather silly, and acknowledged neither one nor the other. How well I remember the Duke of Wellington coming to the orchestra to see this play the night before it was expected the Whigs would go out. I daresay he knew little enough what the *Hunchback* was about.

L OOKED at the sun and was satisfied with his promise,
went to bed again and slept till half past eight. At
eleven Pendleton Hosack came for me. We adjourned to
Warren Street, where were assembled all the party. Our
steeds having arrived, we mounted and began to progress.
Mr. and Mrs. Alexander Hosack followed in the stanhope.
Then came a wagon, containing a negro servant, Neptune,
and sundry baskets of champagne, cake and cherry bounce.
Away we rushed down Broadway, to the infinite edifica-
tion of the gaping multitudes. Mr. Hosack had gotten me
a enchanting horse that trotted like an angel. So in spite
of Major Wilkes' denunciation of "disgusting", I had a hard
trot through all the streets, rising in my saddle like a lady,
or rather, a gentleman. My habit seemed to excite condi-
derable admiration and approbation.

We crossed the Brooklyn ferry in the steamboat and
landed safely on the other side. The whole army defiled—
the stanhope taking the van, the horses forming the main
body and the provisions bringing up the rear. Those Hosacks
are a charming family, for Mrs. Hosack sits straight in her
saddle, and the Doctor settled before we started, that when
we had despatched his patients, he would call for Dall in
his gig, and come down to meet us at the fort. Our ride
thither was extremely aggreeable, the day was clear, cold
and grey, a delightful day for riding. We reached the fort,
the narrows and the Sandy Hook lighthouse. Then we went
over the fort. 'Tis a fortification of no great size or strength,
I should think. But its position, which commands the narrow entrance to the bay of New York, effectually guards the
watery defile that leads to the city of mammon. We looked
at the guns and powder magazine, walked round the walls
and peeped into the officers' quarters, and then descended

to seek where we might eat. We knocked up the quarters of an old woman who kept a cottage, good enough for our purpose. We got sundry logs of wood, and made a blazing fire, the baskets were opened, and soon we presented the interesting spectacle of a dozen people each with a lump of cake in one hand a champagne glass in the other. Mr. Cochrane and Mrs. Hosack stuck to the cherry bounce.

We remounted and set off for home by another road—a very lovely one, all along the riverside. Ere we had progressed long, we met Dall and Dr. Hosack in the gig. The nice good man had kept his work and gone to fetch her. Came home at full speed, and arrived at half past four, having ridden, I should think, nearly twenty miles.

After dinner pottered about, played the piano till nine, when we adjourned to the Hones. Dr. Wainwright was there, whom I was glad to see, and also that Mrs. Charles Augustus Davis, who is utter horror and perturbation of spirit to me. After a little time, dancing was proposed, and I stood up with Mr. Robert Emmett, who observed that Dr. Wainwright had gone, as he chose never to be present while waltzing was going on. I felt shocked that unconsciously I should have been instrumental in driving him away, and much surprised that those who knew of his disapprobation of waltzing, should have proposed it. However, he had gone, and did not return. So I waltzed myself out of my remorse. I danced sundry quadrilles and finally, what they call a Kentucky reel, and what is nothing more than Sir Roger de Coverly turned Backwoodsman. Finally, at one o'clock, came home, having danced myself fairly off my legs.

Thursday, November 22nd

IT poured with rain all day. Dr. Wainwright called and gave me a sermon about waltzing. As it was perfectly good sense, I promised him never to waltz again, except with a woman or with my brother. After all, it is not fitting that a man should put his arm round one's waist. 'Tis much against what I have always thought most sacred—the dignity of a woman in her own eyes and those of others. I like Dr. Wainwright most exceedingly. After saying that he felt convinced from conversations he had heard amongst men, that waltzing was immoral in its tendency, he added, "I am married and have been in love, and cannot imagine anything more destructive of the deep and devoted respect which love is calculated to excite in every honourable man's heart, than to see any and every impertinent coxcomb in a ballroom, come up to her, and, without remorse or hesitation, clasp her waist, imprison her hand, and whirl her around the room." So spake the good Dr. So farewell, sweet German waltz! next to hock, the most intoxicating growth of the Rhineland. I shall never keep time to your pleasant measure again!—no matter.

After dinner received a pretty anonymous nosegay, with very flattering doggrel. The play was *The Stranger*. It poured cats and dogs and the streets were all grey pudding. I did not expect to see six people in the house, instead of which, it was crowded. A satisfactory proof of our attraction.

Saturday, November 24th

OUR riding expedition having been put off, the day was beautifully bright and clear. Went out with my father down to the tailor's to upbraid him about my waistcoat, which is infamously ill-made. The various censures which travellers have bestowed upon various things in this country, are constantly, both in private conversation and the public prints, attributed to *English jealousy*. I confess I have been amused at the charge, and only hope that I may not draw down so awful an accusation on myself, when I declare, that during a three years' residence in America, almost every article, of every description, which I have had made, has been ill-made, and obliged to undergo manifold alterations.

Dressed for dinner at the Hones. Mme. Cochrane did not sent my gown home in time—abominable sempstress! so put on my blue and looked rather dowdy. After dinner the party became much larger. Presently three men sang that sea glee that I remember Lord and Lady Ellesmere teaching me at Oatlands. By and by, dancing was proposed, and I was much entreated and implored to change my determination about waltzing. But I was inexorable, and waltzed only with ladies, who one and all, dance extremely well.

On my return home found my black satin gown, every atom of which will have to be unpicked! The trades-people here are really terrible, they can do nothing, and will take no pains to do anything. 'Tis a handsome gown spoilt. When you carry your complaint of careless work, or want of punctuality to the trades-people you employ here, the unfortunate principals really excite your sympathy by their helpless situation with regard to the free republicans whom they employ, and who, come when they please, depart when they like, work when they choose, and if you remonstrate, take themselves off to new masters, secure of employment in your neighbour's house, if your mode of employing them displeases them. Manifold are the lamentations I have heard of—"Oh, ma'am, this is not like the old country. We can't get journeymen to work here, ma'am, we're obliged to do just as our workmen please!". One poor French dress-maker appeared to be on the verge of distraction, from the utter impossibility of keeping in order a tribe of sewing girls, whom she seemed to pay on purpose that they might drive her crazy. Patience is the only remedy. Whoever lives here, that has ever lived elsewhere, should come provided with it.

YESTERDAY was evacuation day, but as yesterday was the Lord's day also, the American militia army postponed their yearly exhibition, and instead of rushing about the streets in token of their thankfulness at the departure of the British, they quietly went to church, and praised God for the same. Today, however, we have had some firing of pop-guns, waving of star-spangled banners (some of them rather the worse for wear), infantry marching through the streets, cavalry, (Oh Lord! what delicious objects they were!), and artillery prancing along with them, to the infinite ecstacy and peril of a dense mob. Went to rehearsal at half past ten. We were detained a full ten minutes on the way thither, by the defiling of troops, who were progressing down Broadway.

After rehearsal came home, and Mr. Ogden Hoffman called. We spent a delightful half hour at the window, which overlooked the park, commanded a full view of the military marshalled there. They were certainly not quite so bad as Falstaff's men of ragged memory—perhaps all of them had shirts to their backs. But some had gloves and some had not; some carried their guns one way and some another; some had caps of one fashion and some of another; some had no caps at all, but shocking bad hats with feathers in them. The infantry were, however, comparatively respectable troops. They did not march many degrees out of the straight line, or stoop too much, or turn round their heads too often.

But the cavalry! oh the cavalry! what gems without price they were! Apparently extremely frightened at the shambling tituppy chargers upon whose backs they clung, straggling in all directions, putting the admiring crowd in fear of their lives, and proving beyond a doubt how formidable they must appear to the enemy, when, with the most peaceable intentions, they thus jeopardised the safety of their enthusiastic fellow-citizens. Bold would have been the man who did not edge backwards into the crowd, as a flock of these worthies on horse-back came down the street, some trotting, some galloping, some ambling, each and all "witching the world with wondrous horsemanship".

If anything might be properly be called wondrous, the riders and their accoutrements deserve that title. Some wore boots, some wore shoes, and one independent hero had on grey stockings and slippers! Some had bright yellow feathers, and some red and black feathers. I remember particularly, a doctor in a black suit, Hessian boots, a cocked hat and bright yellow guantlets. Another fellow was dressed in the costume of one of *Der Freischutz's* corps—it looked for all the world like a fancy dress parade.

The bands of these worthies were worthy of them. Half a dozen fifers and drummers playing old English jig tunes. In spite of the injustice of such a comparison, I could not keep out of my head the last soldiers I had seen, those fine tall fellows, the Grenadier Guards, that used to delight us of a Sunday morning in St. James Park, and their exquisite band and dandy-looking officers. These *looked* like soldiers, whatever they might fight like.

I sat writing to Harriet till time to go to the theatre. The play was *Isabella*, the house crammed, a regular holiday audience, shrieking, shouting, laughing, like one of our Christmas pantomimes. I acted like a wretch. My dress looked very handsome, particularly my marriage dress. But my muslin bed-gown was so long that I set my feet through it the very first thing. And then those "animaux bêtes" who dragged me off, tore a beautiful point lace veil I had on to tatters, a thing that cost three guineas, if a farthing!

XI

An invitation to act in Jamaica—A visit to "Hell-gate"—A party at the James Bells'—Loud voices of American women—the American version of the quadrille—A visit to Mr. Grant Thorburn—Dinner at the Hosacks

Monday, November 26th, 1832

MY father received a most amusing letter this morning from Lord Mulgrave, asking us to come over to Jamaica to act, offering us quarters in his house, and plenty of volunteer actors (did he include himself, I wonder?), to make up a company, if we will come. I should like it very well. To pass the winter in that nice warm climate would be delightful, and I dare say we would find our stay there amusing and agreeable enough. I wish we could do it.

Tuesday, November 27th, 1832

AT half past twelve went out with my father and Colonel Sibell. Called upon his honour, the Recorder, but he was in court and was not to be seen. Walked down to the Battery. The day was most lovely like an early day in June in England, and I was obliged to take my parasol with me, the sun was so hot. The Battery was as usual, totally deserted, though the sky, and the shores and the beautiful bright bay were smiling in perfect loveliness. A delicious fresh breeze came wandering over the wide estuary, and graceful boats with their full sails glittering in the sun, glided to and fro, like summer clouds across the blue heavens. The river craft hovering from morning till night along the waters that surround New York, must be the most beautiful in the world. Their lightness, grace, swiftness and strength appear to me to be unequalled. Such beautiful vessels I never saw, more beautiful ones I cannot imagine.

Came home at half past one. Mr. Bell called with one Mr. Sedgwick, kinsman to the authoress, Catherine Sedgwick. While they were here, Mrs. Hosack called to settle about tomorrow's ride. At half past five went to the theatre. Play, *The Gamester*—my father's benefit; the house was very good. I played pretty well.

Wednesday, November 28th

AFTER breakfast sat reading the poems of Willis, a young man whose works, young as they evidently are, would have won him some consideration in any but such a thorough work-a-day world as this. I cried a good deal over some of this man's verses—I thought some of them beautiful. I think all things are sad. 'Tis sad to hear sweet music; 'tis sad to read fine poetry; 'tis sad to look upon the beautiful face of a fair woman; 'tis sad to behold the unclouded glory of a summer's sky. I remember when I first recited Juliet to my mother, she said I spoke the Balcony scene almost sadly. Was not such deep, deep love so strong, too passionate, too pervading, to be uttered with the light laughing voice of pleasure? was not that love even in its fulness of joy, sad—awful? However, perhaps I do but see through my own medium, and fancy it is the universal one.

At about twelve o'clock, Mrs. Pendleton Hosack called for me, and escorted by her husband and Mr. Emmett, we rode forth to visit the island. We went to a pretty cottage belonging to Mr. Emmett's father-in-law, Dr. Hosack. The day was still and grey—a pleasant day, but there was no sunshine, but neither were there any dark shadows. My horse had been ill ridden by somebody or other, and was mighty disagreable. Our ride was pleasant enough. Masses of granite and greenish basalt, wild underwood, and vivid cedar bushes. The Hudson lay leaden and sullen under the wings of the restless wind. We stood to hear the delicious music of water plashing against the rocky shore, which is the pleasantest sound in the world. We then rode to a place yclept Hell Gate, from a dangerous current in the East river, where ships have been lost. The ladies of New York, and all lady-like superior people, have agreed to call this eddy, Hurlgate. The superior propriety of this name is not to be questioned, for hell is a shocking bad word, no doubt, but being infinitely more appropriate to the place and its qualities, I have ventured to mention it. Came home a little past four, and devoured sundry puddings and pies.

After dinner strummed on the piano till eight, then dressed and off to Mrs. Bell's—"a small party, my dear". Mr. Sedgwick was there; I like him, he has something in him, and is not vulgar or impertinent. Was introduced to a very handsome French Creole woman whom I liked. She reminded me of my mother, and her son bore a striking resemblance to dear John, my brother. The ladies here have an extreme aversion to being called *women*, I don't exactly understand why. Their idea is that that term designates only the lower or less refined classes of female human-kind. This is a mistake which I wonder they should fall into. In all countries in the world, queens, duchesses, and countesses are called *women*. But in this one alone, washerwomen, sempstresses, and housemaids are called *ladies,* so that in fact here, woman is by far the most desirable appelation of the two.

The women's voices here distract me, so loud, so rapid and with such a twang! What a pity! for they are, almost without exception, lovely-looking creatures, with an air of refinement in their appearance, which would be very attractive, but for their style of dress and those tremendous shrill, loud voices. This terrible nuisance has often made me wish for that "still small voice" which has become the universal tone of good society in England, and which, however inconvenient sometimes from its utter inaudibility, at least did not send one to bed with one's ears ringing, and one's head splitting.

I was in a society of about twelve ladies the other evening, and the uproar was so excessive that I felt my eyebrows contracting from a sense of perfect bewilderment, occasioned by the noise all around me, and more than once I was obliged to request the person with whom I was conversing to stop till the noise had subsided a little, that I might be able to distinguish what he was saying to me. Were the women here large and masculine in appearance, this defect would appear less strange, though no less disagreable. But they are singularly delicate and feminine in their style of beauty, and the noise they make strikes one with surprise as something monstrous and unnatural—like mice roaring. They frequently talk four or five at a time, and directly across each other, neither of which proceedings are exactly according to my ideas of good breeding.

Later that evening at the Bells', we stood up to dance a couple of quadrilles. But as they had not one distinct idea of what the figures were, the whole was a mess of running about, explaining, jostling and awkward blundering. The established succession of figures which form the one French quadrille, in executing which the ballrooms of Paris and London have spent so many satisfactory hours, ever since it was invented, by no means satisfies the Americans. At the close of almost every quadrille, a *fancy* figure is danced, which, depending entirely upon the directions of the leader of the band, is a very curious medley of all the rest. The company not being gifted with second sight, and of course not knowing at every step what next they may be called upon to do, fearfully sliding along, looking at each other, asking "how does it go on?", the whole being a complete confusion of purpose and execution. I took greatly to the governness of the family, a German woman, with a right German face, a nice person, with quiet simple manners. Came home at twelve o'clock. My favourite aversion, Mrs. Charles Augustus Davis was there.

Thursday, November 29th

MY father has received a most comical note from one Grant Thorburn, a Scotch gardener, florist and seedsman. The note expresses a great desire that my father and myself will call upon him, for that he wishes very much to look at us, that the hours of the theatre are too late for him, and that besides, he wants to see us as ourselves, and not as "kings and princesses". I have entreated my father to go; this man must be worth knowing—I shall certainly keep his note.

Friday, November 30th

HOW the time goes! bless the old traveller, how he posts along! After breakfast Mrs. James Bell and her son called, and Mr. Sedgwick called. I like the latter; his manners are very good, and he is altogether more like a gentleman than most men here. When they were gone, walked out with my father to Grant Thorburn's. The day was grey and cold and damp—a real November day, such as we know them. We held the good man's note and steered our course by it. In the process of time we entered a garden, passed through a greenhouse, and arrived at an immense and most singularly arranged seed-shop, with galleries running round it, and the voice of a hundred canaries resounding through it. I don't know why, but it reminded me of a place in the Arabian Nights. "Is Mr. Thorburn within?", shouted my father, seeing no one in this strange abode. "Yes, he is!", was replied from somewhere by somebody. We looked about, and presently, with his little grey bullet head, and shrewd piercing eyes, just appearing above the counter, we detected the master of the house. My father stepped up to him with an air like the Duke of Wellington, and returning his coarse, curiously folded note to him, said, "I presume I am addressing Mr. Thorburn?, this sir," drawing me forward, "is Miss Fanny Kemble". The little man snatched off his spectacles, rushed round the counter, rubbed his enormous hand upon his blue stuff apron, and held it out to us with a most hearty welcome. He looked at us for some time, and then exclaimed—"Ha! ye're her father? Well, ye'll have married pretty early—ye look very young, I should not have been sae much surprised if ye had called her ye're wife!" I laughed and my father smiled at this compliment, which was recommended by a broad Scotch twang, which always sounds sweetly in my ears.

The little man, whose appearance is that of a dwarf in some fairy tale, then went to tell us how Galt had written a book all about him; how it was almost word for word his own story; how he had come to this country in early life with three half pence in his pocket, and a nail and a hammer in his hand for all wordly substance. How he had earned his bread by making nails, which was his business in Scotland. How one day, passing some flowers exposed for sale, he had touched a geranium leaf by accident, and charmed by its fragrance, bought it, never having seen one before. With fifteen dollars in his pocket, he commenced the business of florist and gardener, and had refused as many thousand dollars for his present prosperous concern. When he first came to New York, the place opposite his garden, where now stands a handsome modern dwelling-house, was the site of a shed where he did his first bit of work.

After six-and-twenty years absence from Scotland, he returned home. He told how he came to his father's house— "'Twas on a bright morning in August, it was, when I went through the door. I knew all the old passages so well. I opened the parlour door, and there, according to the good old Scottish custom, the family were going to prayers afore breakfast. There was the old Bible on the table, and the old clock ticking away in the corner of the room. There was my father in his own old chair, exactly where I had left him six-and-twenty years gone by. The very shovel and tongs by the fire were the same, I knew them all. I just sat down, and cried as sweetly as ever man did in his life".

These were, as nearly as I can recollect, his words—and oh! what a story! His manner too, was indescribably vivid and graphic. My father's eyes filled with tears. He stretched out his hand and shook the Scotchman's hand repeatedly without speaking. I never saw him more excited. I was never more struck myself with the wonderful strangeness of this bewildering life. He showed us the foot of a rude rustic-looking table. "That", he said, "was cut from the hawthorn hedge that grows by my father's house; and this," showing us a wooden bowl, "is what I take my *parritch* in!" I asked him if he never meant to leave this country and to return to bonny Scotland? He said—no, never. He might return, but he never meant to settle anywhere but here. "For", added he, "I have grown what I am in it, madam, and 'tis a fine country for the poor." I could have listened to this strange oracle for a day, but in the midst of his discourse, he was summoned to dinner—and presenting his son to us, who presented a nosegay to me, left us to wander about his singular domain. We walked about the shop, visited the birds, who are taken most admirable care of, and are extremely beautiful. Saw an English blackbird and a thrush, in *cages*— they made my heart ache. I wonder if they ever think of the ripe red cracking cherries, the rich orchard lands, and the hawthorn-hedged lanes in the summer sunsets of dear England?—I did it for them. After dawdling about very satisfactorily for some time, we departed.

At five my father and I went to Mrs. Hosack's—a pleasant dinner. I like him enough and I like her very much. She is extremely pretty and very pleasant. After dinner, the usual entertaining half hour among the ladies passed in looking over caricatures. When the men joined us, Mr. Alexander Hosack came and sat down by me, and in the course of a few minutes, we fell into English talk. It appears that he knows sundry of my gracious patrons, among the rest the Wiltons. He had been at Heaton, and it pleased me to speak of it again. But what in the name of all wonders could possess him with the idea that Lady St. Maur was guilty of editing the comic annual? Was asked to sing, and sang "Ah no ben mio", pretty well. Mr. Ogden Hoffman sang a thing of his own very well, though it was not in itself worth much. Discussed all manner of prima donnas with him.

At half past nine, Dall came for me, and we proceeded to the Hones. The people here never tell one when they mean to dance, the consequence is that one is completely put out about one's toilet. I was in a black satin dress, and dancing in these hot rooms, might as well have been in a pall. The room was full of pretty women, each one prettier than the other. I danced myself half dead, and came home. By the by, Mrs. Hone's bedroom where we left our cloaks, made my heart ache. 'Twas exactly like my dear little bedroom at home, the bed, the furniture, and the rose-coloured lining, all the same.

XII

*Journey from New York to Philadelphia—Reflections on the
independence of shop-keepers and servants—"How I do loathe my most
impotent and unpoetical craft!"—A walk to Fair Mount bridge—A
ride to Laurel Hill with Pierce Butler—First night of* The Wonder—
To Laurel Hill again with Mr. Staley this time

Saturday, December 1st, 1832

F IRST day of the last month of the year—go to it old
fellow! I'm sick of the road, and would be at my journey's end. Got two hundred dollars from my father, and after breakfast sallied forth, paid bills and visits and came
home. Found my father sitting with our kinsman, Governor Kemble, busily discussing the family origin, root,
branches and all. We are an old family, they say, but the
direct line is lost after Charles the Second's reign. Our
kinsman is a nice man, with a remarkably fine face, with
which I was greatly struck. When he was gone, I persuaded
my father to come down and take a breathing on the Battery with me. And a breathing it was with a vengeance.
The wind blew tempestuously, the waters, all troubled and
rough, were of a yellow green colour, breaking into short,
angry waves, whose glittering white crests the wind carried
away as they sank to the level surface again. The shores
were all cold, distinct, sharp-cut and wintry-looking, the
sky was black and gloomy, with now and then a watery
sunlight running through it. The wind was so powerful, we
could scarcely keep our legs. My sleeves and skirts fluttered
in the blast, my bonnet was turned from part behind, my
nose was blue, my cheeks were crimson, my hair was all

tangled, my breath was gone, my blood was in a glow—
what a walk! Met dear Dr. Wainwright, whom I love. Came
in—dined.

After dinner, bethought me that I had not called upon
Mrs. Sibell, according to promise. Sent for a coach, and set
forth thither. Didn't know the number, so drove up Spring
Street, and down Spring Street, and finally stopped at a shop
and got a directory and found the address. Sat a few minutes with her and at five o'clock left her. The day was already gone—the gloaming come. The keen cutting wind
whizzed along the streets, the moon was up, clear, cold and
radiant; the crowd had ebbed away from the busy thoroughfare, and only a few men in great coats buttoned up to
their chins, and women wrapped in cloaks, were scudding
along in the dim twilight and the bitter wind towards their
several destinations, with a frozen shuddering look that made
me laugh. I had got perished in the coach, and seeing that
the darkness covered me, determined to walk home and bade
the coach follow me. How pleasant it was; I walked tremendously fast, enjoying the fresh wind of the north, and
looking at the glittering moon as she rode high in the evening sky. How I do like walking alone—being alone, for
this I wish I were a man.

At half past five went to the theatre—play, *The Hunchback*. I missed Ogden Hoffman from his accustomed seat,
and found that like a politician he had changed sides. I
played abominably, my voice was weak and fagged. After
the play, Katharine and Petruchio. I played that better, my
father was admirable—it went off delightfully. When it was
over they called for my father, and with me in his hand,
he went on. The pit rose to us like Christians and shouted
and halloed as I have been used to hear. I felt sorry to leave
them, they are a pleasant audience to act to, and exceedingly civil to us and I have got rather attached to them.

New York seems nearer home than any other place, and I felt sorry to leave it. When we had withdrawn and were going upstairs, we heard three distinct cheers. On asking what that meant, we learnt 'twas a compliment to us—thank 'em kindly.

Sunday, November 2nd

SWALLOWED two mouthfuls of bread and away to church. It was very crowded and a worthy woman had taken possession of the corner seat in Mr. Hone's pew, with a fidgetting little child, which she kept dancing up and down every two minutes. Though in church I wished for the days of King Herod.

Came home and found a whole regiment of men. His honour the Recorder, who is my special delight, Mr. Sedgwick, whom I greatly affection, to these presently entered Mr. Wilkes and Mr. Cochrane. They one by one bade me good-by. Mr. Wilkes read me a passage out of one of Jeffrey's letters describing an English fine lady. The picture is admirable and most faithful. They are indeed, polished, brilliant, smooth as ice, as slippery, as treacherous, as cold. When they were all gone, Colonel Sibell gave me to read the descriptive sketch of the French opera, *La Tentation*, that has been setting all Paris wild. What an atrocious piece of blasphemy, indecency and folly—what a thoroughly French invention. Mad people! mad people!

Monday, December 3rd

ROSE at half past four. The sky was as black as death, but in the night winter had dropped his mantle on the earth, and there it lay, cold and purely white, against the inky sky. In thaw, sleet and rain, drove down to the steamboat. Went directly to the cabin, but on my way thither, managed to fall down half a dozen steps and give myself as many bruises. I was picked up and led to a bed, where I slept profoundly till breakfast time. Our kinsman, Governor Kemble, was our fellow passenger, I like him mainly. After breakfast returned to my crib. As I was removing my book in order to lie down, a lady said to me, "Let me look at one of those books", and without further word of question or acknowledgement, took it from my hand and began reading. I was a little surprised, but said nothing, and went to sleep. Presently I was roused by a pull on the shoulder, and another lady, rather more civil, asked me to do her the favour of lending her the other book. I said by all manner of means, wished her at the devil, and turned round to sleep once more.

Arrived at Amboy, we disembarked and bundled ourselves into our coach, ourselves, our namesake, and a pretty quiet lady who was going with much heaviness to see a sick child. The roads were unspeakable. My bruises made the saltatory movements of our crazy conveyance doubly torturing—in short, all things were the perfection of misery. I attempted to read, but found it impossible to do so. Arrived at the Delaware, we took boat again. As I was sitting very quietly reading, with another volume lying on the stool at my feet, the same unceremonious lady who had borrowed it before, snatched it up without addressing a single word to me, read as long as she pleased, and threw it down again in the same style when she went in to dinner. Now I know that half the people here would say, "Oh, but you know she could not have been a lady; 'tis not fair to judge our manners by the vulgar specimens of American society which a steamboat may afford." Very true, but granting she was *not* a lady (which she certainly was not), supposing her to have been a housemaid, or anything else of equal pretensions to good breeding, the way to judge is by comparing her, not with ladies in other countries, but with housemaids, persons in her own conditions of life, and 'tis most certain that no person whatsoever, however ignorant, low, or vulgar, in England, would have done such a thing as that.

The mixture of the republican feeling of equality peculiar to this country, and the usual want of refinement common to the lower classes of most countries, forms a singularly felicitious union of impudence and vulgarity to be met with no where but in America. Americans are indeed independent. Every man that will work a little can live extremely well. No portion of the country is yet overstocked with followers of trades, not even the Atlantic cities. Living is cheap, labour is dear. To conclude, as the Irish woman said, "It is a darling country for poor folks. If I worked three days in the week, can't I lie in my bed the other three if I please?"

Two circumstances which have come to my knowledge, will serve to illustrate the spirit of the people. A farmer who is in the habit of calling at our house on his way to market, with eggs, poultry, etc., being questioned as to whether the eggs were new-laid, replied—"No, not the *very* fresh ones, we eat all those ourselves".

On returning home from the theatre one night, I could not find my slippers anywhere. The next morning, on inquiring of the maid if she knew anything of them, she replied with perfect equanimity, that having walked home through the snow, and got her feet very wet, she had put them on, and forgotten to return them to their place before my return. Nobody, I think, will doubt that an English farmer, and an English servant, might sell stale eggs, and use their mistress's slippers, but I think it doubtful if either fact would have been acknowledged with such perfect honesty anywhere but here.

Arrived at the Mansion House, Philadelphia, which I was quite glad to see again. Stowed away my things, made a delicious huge wood fire, dressed myself, and went down to dinner. Our kinsman dined with us. Mr. Pierce Butler came in while we were at dinner. After dinner came up to my room, and continued unpacking and putting away my things. When we went down to tea, my father was lying on the sofa asleep, and a man was sitting with his back to the door, reading the newspaper. He looked up as we came in—it was Mr. Staley, whom I greatly rejoiced to see again. During tea, he told us all the Philadelphia gossip. So the ladies are all getting up upon horses, and wearing the "Kemble" cap, as they call Lady Ellesmere's device. How she would laugh if she could hear it, and how I did laugh when I did hear it. The Kemble cap, forsooth!

Tuesday, December 4th

AFTER breakfast practised for two hours. Mr. Staley called and stayed some time. Came up to my room, when a note containing two cards, and an invitation to "tea" from Miss Chapman's, was brought to me. Presently I was called down to receive our kinsman, who sat some time with me, and whom I like most especially, who is a gentleman and a very nice person. Came up and resumed my journal, and was again summoned down to see young Mr. Biddle. When he was gone, finished journal, wrote to my mother, read a canto in Dante, and began to write a novel.

Dined at five, and at a quarter to ten, went to the theatre for my father. I had on the same dress I wore at Devonshire House, the night of the last ball I was at in England, and looked at myself in amazement, to think of all the strangenesses that have befallen since then. We proceeded to Miss Chapman's, and this tea party turned out to be a very crowded dance, in small rooms, upon carpets, and with the roasting fire. Was introduced to all the world and his wife. Came away a little after twelve. I never felt anything like the heat of the rooms, nor heard anything so strange as the questions the people ask one, or saw anything more lovely than the full moonlight on the marble buildings of Philadelphia.

Wednesday, December 5th

AFTER breakfast, practised; Mr. and Mrs. Nicholas Biddle called, also Dr. Charles Mifflin. Went and saw poor Mrs. Dulaney, she interests me most extremely, I like her very very much. Came up to my room and read a canto of Dante. Was called down to see folk, and found the drawing room literally thronged. The first face I made out was Mr. Kemble's, for whom I have taken a special love, two ladies, a whole load of men, and Mr. Edward Biddle, who had brought me a curious piece of machinery in the shape of a musical box, to look at. It contained a little bird, with golden and purple wings, and a tiny white beak. On the box being wound up, this little creature flew out, began fluttering its wings, opening its beak, and uttering sundry very melodious warblings, in the midst of which, it sank suddenly down and disappeared, the lid closed and there was an end!

At half past five went to the theatre. The play was *Romeo and Juliet,* the house not good. I acted like a wretch, of course, how could I do otherwise? Oh Juliet! vision of the south! rose of the garden of the earth! was this the glorious hymn that Shakespeare hallowed to your praise? How I do loathe the stage! these wretched, tawdry, glittering rags, flung over the breathing forms of ideal loveliness. These miserable, poor and pitiful substitutes for the glories with which poetry has invested her magnificent and fair creations! What a mass of wretched mumming mimicry acting is. Pasteboard and paint for the thick breathing orange groves of the south; green silk and oiled parchment for the so-called splendour of the noon; wooden platforms and canvas curtains for the solid marble balconies, and rich dark draperies of Juliet's sleeping chamber, that shrine of love and beauty; rouge, for the startled life-blood in the cheek of that young passionate woman; an actress, a mimicker, a sham creature, me, in fact, or any other one, for that loveliest and most wonderful conception, in which all that is true in nature, and all that is exquisite in fancy, are moulded into a living form. To *act* this! to *act Romeo and Juliet!*—horror! horror! how I do loathe my most impotent and unpoetical craft!

In the last scene of the play, I was so mad with the mode in which all the preceding ones had been perpetrated, that lying over Romeo's corpse, and fumbling for his dagger, which I could not find, I, Juliet, thus apostrophised him, Romeo being dead—"Why, where the devil is your dagger?" What a disgusting travesty. On my return home I expressed my determination to my father to perform the farce of Romeo and Juliet no more. Why, it's an absolute shame that one of Shakespeare's plays should be thus turned into a mockery. I received a note from young Mr. Biddle, accompanied by a very curious nosegay in shells; a poor substitute for the breathing fresh, rosy flowers he used to furnish me with, when I was last here.

Thursday, December 6th

THE morning was beautifully bright and warm, like a May morning in England. After breakfast practised for two hours, and then was summoned to see my kinsman, who sat some time, and whom I like of all things. He makes out (for he seems a great meddler in these matters), that we are originally Italian people, pirates, by name, Campo Bello; the same family as the Scottish Campbells and the Norman Beauchamps; how I wish it were true!

I sat watching the glorious sunset as it came redly streaming into my room, touching everything with glory, and shining through my hair upon my book. After dinner, sat writing my journal till ten, when my father returned. The moon was shining soft and full, and he asked me if I would take a walk. I bonneted and booted, and we sallied forth to the Schuylkill. The moon withdrew herself behind a veil of thin white clouds, but left a clear grey light over the earth. We reached the Fair Mount bridge at about eleven. The turnpike was fast and everybody asleep, so we climbed over the gate, and very deliberately pursued our way through the strange dark-looking covered bridge, where the glimmering lamps at distant intervals, threw the crossing beams and rafters into momentary brightness, that had a strange effect contrasted with the surrounding gloom. The bridges here are all made of wood, and for the most part covered. The one-arched bridge at Fair Mount is particularly light and graceful in its appearance. At a distance, it looks like a scarf, rounded by the wind, flung over the river.

We reached the other side, and turning off the road, began climbing the hill opposite the breakwater. The road was muddy in the valley with the heavy rains, and unwilling to wade through the dirt, we clambered along a paling for several yards, and so escaped the mire. My father steered for the grassy knoll just opposite Fair Mount, and there, screened by a thicket of young cedar bushes, with the river breaking over the broad dam far below us, we sat down on a tree trunk. Here we remained for upwards of quarter of an hour without uttering a syllable—indeed we had not spoken three words since we set out. We were disturbed by a large white spaniel dog, who, coming down from among the cedar bushes, reminded us of the old witch stories. We arose to depart, and took our way towards the Market Street bridge, along the banks of the river. The moon, faintly struggling through the clouds, now touched the dark pyramids of the cedar trees that rose up into the grey sky, and threw our shadows on the lonely path we were pursuing. The air was soft and balmy as the night air of mid August. The world was still, and except for our footfalls as we trudged along, no sound disturbed the universal repose. We did not reach home till half twelve.

As we walked down Market Street, through the long ranges of casks, the only creatures stirring, except some melancholy, night-loving cats, my father said very calmly—"How I do wish I had a gimlet", "What for?"—"What fun it would be to pierce every one of these barrels". For a gentleman of his years, this appeared to me rather a juvenile prompting of Satan; and as I laughlingly expostulated on the wickedness of such a proceeding, he replied with much innocence, "I don't think they'd ever suspect me of having done it", and truly, I don't think they would. Came home and went to bed. That was a curious fancy of my father's.

Friday, December 7th

FOUND Pierce Butler in the breakfast room. The morning was very unpropitious, but I settled to ride at one, if it was tolerably fine then. He remained pottering a long time; when he was gone, went in for a few minutes to Mrs. Dulaney. At one the horses came, but mine was brought without a stirrup, so we had to wait till the blundering groom had ridden back for it. At length we mounted.

"Handsome is as handsome does" is verity, and therefore, pretty as was my steed, I wished its good looks and itself at the devil, before I was half way down Chestnut Street. It pranced, and danced, and backed me once right upon the pavement. We took the Laurel Hill road. The days was the perfection of gloom—the road six inches deep in heavy mud. We walked the whole way out—my father got the cramp and lost his temper. At Laurel Hill we dismounted and walked down to the river side. How melancholy it all looked; the turpid rhubarby water, the skeleton woods, the grey sky, and far winding away of the rocky shores, yet it was fine even in this gloom and wonderfully still.

Pierce Butler and I scrambled down the rocks towards the water, expatiating on the capabilities of the place, which was once a country seat, and with very little expense might be made a very comfortable as well as a very enchanting residence. Always expecting of course, the chance of fever and ague during the summer months, when the whole of the banks of the Schuylkill, high and rocky as they are, are considered so unhealthy that the inhabitants are obliged to leave their houses till the winter season, when the country naturally loses half its attractions.

At half past three we mounted, and crossing the river, returned home by a much better route. My horse, however, was decidedly a brute—pulled my arms to pieces, cantered with the wrong leg foremost, trotted in a sort of scuttling fashion, that rendered it utterly impossible to rise in the stirrups, and instead of walking, jogged the breath out of my body. I was fairly done up when we reached home. Pierce Butler dined with us.

After dinner went and sat with Mrs. Dulaney. So it seems, Carolina is in a state of convulsion. Reports have arrived that the Nullifiers and Unionists have had a fight in Charleston, and that lives have been lost. This very crisis (a more important one than has yet occurred in the political existence of this country), is threatening to slacken the bonds of brotherhood between the states, and shake the union to its centre. The interests of the northern states are totally different from, and in some respects opposite to those of the southern states.

The tariff question is the point in debate, and the Carolinians have, it seems, threatened to secede from the Union in consequence of the policy pursued with regard to that. I was horrified at Dr. Charles Mifflin's account of the state of the negroes in the south. To teach a slave to read or write is to incur a penalty either of fine or imprisonment. They form the larger part of the population by far, and so great is the dread of insurrection on the part of the white inhabitants, that they are kept in the most brutal ignorance, and too often treated with the most brutal barbarity, in order to ensure their subjection. Oh! what a breaking asunder of old manacles there will be, some of these fine days; what a fearful rising of the black flood; what a sweeping away, as by a torrent, of oppressions and tyrannies; what a fierce and horrible retaliation and revenge for a wrong so long endured, so wickedly inflicted.

Wednesday, December 12th

AFTER breakfast, went to rehearsal. It poured with rain. Came home, finished letter to Harriet, wrote journal, dined at three. After dinner, went and sat with Mrs. Dulaney. Sang to her all my old Scottish ballads, and read the first act of *The Hunchback* to her. At half past five went to the theatre. Play *King John,* house good, I played horribly. My voice was tired with my exertions, and cracked most awfully. I finished early, and came home in my dress to show Mrs. Dulaney. Sat talking to her till my father came home.

So "Old Hickory" means to lick the refractory southerners; why are they coming to a civil war? However, the grumblers haven't the means of fighting without emancipating and arming their slaves. That they will not and dare not do. The consequence will be, I suppose, that they will swallow the affront and submit.

Thursday, December 13th

AT half past twelve set off with Dall to the riding school. It was full of women in long calico skirts and gay bonnets with flaunting feathers, riding like wretches. I put on a skirt and my riding cap, and mounted a rough, rugged, white brown beast, that looked more like an old trunk than anything else, its coat standing literally on end with heat and ill condition. 'Tis vain attempting to ride like a Christian on these heathen horses, which are neither broken, bitted, nor bridled properly. The poor dumb creatures have no more idea of what a horse ought to be, or how a horse ought to behave, than so many cows. My hair, with the damp and the shaking, became perfectly straight. I asked for Tuesday's charger, and the school having by degrees got empty, I managed to become a little better acquainted with its ways. 'Tis a pretty little creature, but 'tis not half broken, is horribly ill ridden, and will never be good for anything. At two o'clock dismounted; Pierce Butler walked home with us. Came to my room, tried on dresses for Lady Macbeth, and *The Wonder*, and dressed for dinner. My father dined out.

Saturday, December 15th

IF I were to write a history of Philadelphia, according to the profound spirit of investigation for which modern tourists are remarkable, I should say that it was a peculiarity belonging to its climate, that Saturday is invariably a wet day. At twelve went to rehearsal after putting out things for the theatre. After rehearsal called at Mr. Sulley's. Saw and carried off his head of me in Juliet. Certainly the resemblance between myself and Mrs. Siddons must be very strong, for this painting might almost have been taken for a copy of Harlowe's sketch of my aunt in Lady Macbeth; 'tis very strange and unaccountable. Came home, wrote journal and went and sat with Mrs. Dulaney till dinner time. After dinner went and sat with her again till coffee time. Was introduced to Dr. Randolph, whom I liked very much. I showed Mrs. Dulaney my dress and bracelets. We had a long discussion about the precedence of one lady before another among the nobility of European courts, whereat her republican pride seemed highly offended. If Clay did, as Dr. Randolph describes, pass before titled men at a dinner in England, with his hands in his breeches' pockets, it only follows thence, that he was really ill-bred, and would be thought vulgar if he did it unwittingly, and absurd if he did it intentionally.

Went to the theatre at half past five. The house was wonderful considering the weather—the play was *Fazio*. I played pretty well—my dress was splendid.

Monday, December 17th

IT poured with rain like the very mischief, a sort of continual gushing down from the clouds, combining all the vehemence of a thunder shower, with all the pertinacity of one of our own November drizzles—delightful! Went to rehearse *Macbeth*. Had a delightful palaver with Mr. Henry Berkley, who knows all the music that was ever writ, and all the singers that ever sang, and worships Pasta as I do.

After dinner went and sat with Mrs. Dulaney till coffee time. At half past five went to the theatre. In spite of the rain the house was very full, and in all my life I never saw so large an assembly of people so perfectly and breathlessly still as they were during several of our scenes. I played like a very clever girl as I am, but it was as much like Lady Macbeth as the Great Mogul.

Tuesday, December 18th

AFTER breakfast went to rehearse *The Wonder*. Called in on my way to Mr. Sulley's who is painting a portrait of my father. Saw one or two lovely women's pictures. I wish he would go to England, I think it would answer his purposes very well. At two went to the riding school, rode till half past three. The day was bitter cold, with a piercing wicked wind riding through the grey sky. Dall and I walked to pay sundry calls. Met Mr. Staley whom he had not seen for two or three days, a most unusual circumstance. He walked home with us. Dall and I dined tete-à-tete. On returning home I found a most lovely nosegay of real, delicious, fragrant flowers. Sweet crimson buds of the faint breathing monthly rose; bright, vivid, dark green myrtle; the honey Daphne Odora, with its clusters of pinky-white blossoms, and the delicate bells of the tall white jasmine—all sweet and living, and fresh, as at midsummer—I was blissful!

After dinner I went in to Mrs. Dulaney, and then came back to the drawing room. Mr. Staley, who had taken the hint about our being alone in the evening, came in. I began making him sing, and taught him "The Leaf and the Fountain". Presently Mr. Pierce Butler was announced—he was the author of the flowers.

WENT to rehearsal—afterwards to the riding school. The school was quite empty and I quite alone. As I was cantering along, amusing myself with cogitations various, Mr. Pierce Butler came in. He stayed the whole time I rode. I settled with him about riding tomorrow, and came home to dinner. After dinner went in to see Mrs. Dulaney, Dr. Randolph was there, who is a remarkably nice man. She is a very delightful person, with a great deal of intellect and a wonderful quantity of fortitude and piety, and a total absence of knowledge of the world, except through books. Her children enchant me, and her care of them enchants me too. She is an excellent person, with a heart overflowing with the very best affections our nature is capable of.

I stayed with her till time to go to the theatre. The house was very full, the play was *The Wonder*—my first time of acting Violante. My dress was not finished till the very last moment—and then, oh horror;! was so small that I could not get into it. It had to be pinned upon me, and thus rebundled, with the dread of cracking my bodice from top to bottom every time I moved, the utter impossibility of drawing breath, from the narrow dimensions into which it squeezed me, I went on to play a new part. The consequence was that I acted infamously, and for the first time in my life was horribly imperfect—out myself, and putting everybody else out. Between every scene my unlucky gown had to be pinned together, and in the laughing scene, it took the hint from my admirable performance, and facetiously grinned in an ecstasy of amusement till it was fairly open behind, displaying, I supposed, the lacing of my stays, like so many teeth, to the admiring gaze of the audience. As I was perfectly ignorant of the circumstances, with my usual easy nonchalance, I persisted in turning by back to the folk, in spite of all my father's pulls and pushes, which I did not comprehend. Pierce Butler was at the play, also Dr. Charles Mifflin, also Henry Clay, who was received with cheers and plaudits manifold. Came home in my dress, and went in to show it to Mrs. Dulaney and her mother, who were both in bed, but marvellously edified by my appearance.

Thursday, December 20th

THE day was beautifully brilliant, clear and cold—winter, but winter in dazzling array of sunshine and crystal; blue skies with light feathery streaks of white clouds running through them; dry, crisp, hard roads, with the delicate rime tipping all the ruts with sparkling jewellery.

After breakfast, Mr. Staley called. I walked out with him to get a cap and whip for Dall. The latter he insisted on making her a present of, and a very pretty one indeed it was, with a delicate ivory handle, and a charming persuading lash. At twelve habited, and helped to equip dear Dall, who looked really exceedingly nice in her jockey habiliments. Went to the school, where we found Mr. Staley waiting for us. Mounted and set forth. We rode out to Laurel Hill. The road was not very good but no mud. Passed that bright youth, Pierce Butler, riding very like an ass on horseback. When we reached Laurel Hill, we dismounted, tied up our horses, and walked first up to that interesting wooden monument, where I inscribed my initials on our first ride thither. Afterwards, Mr. Staley and I scrambled down the rocks to the river side. The water was a broad dazzling river of light, and had a beautiful effect, winding away in brightness that the eye could scarce endure. As I bent over a fine bluff (as they call here any mass of rock standing isolated), I espied below me a natural rocky arch, overhanging the river, all glittering with pure lone diamond icicles. Thither Mr. Staley convoyed me, and broke off one of those wintry gems for me. It measured about two feet long, and was as thick as the root of my wrist. I never saw anything so beautiful as these pendant adornments of the silver-fingered ice god. Toiled up to the house again, where, after brushing our habits, we remounted our chargers and came home.

The river was most beautiful towards the bridge they are building, the unfinished piers of which have a very pretty effect, almost resembling their very opposite, a ruin. The thin, pale vapour of the steam engine, employed in some of the works, rising from the blue water, and rolling its graceful waves far along the dark rocky shore, had a lovely fairy-tale look. While we were at tea, young Edward Biddle and Dr. Mifflin came in. They put me down to the piano, and I continued to sing till past eleven o'clock, when, somebody looking at a watch, there was an exclamation of surprise, the piano was shut down, the gentlemen vanished, and I came to bed.

XIII

The Kemble riding party entertained at Laurel Hill—The drinking
habits of Americans contrasted with those of Englishmen—How the
English celebrate anniversaries—"Acting . . . the very lowest of the
arts"—Journey to Baltimore

December 23rd, Sunday

AFTER church, came home—habited. The villanous
servants did not think fit to announce the horses till
they had been at the door full half an hour, so that when
we started it was near two o'clock. Dall seemed quite at ease
on her gangling charger, and I had gotten up on Mr. Pierce
Butler's big horse to see what I could make of him. The day
was beautifully bright and clear, with a warm blessed sunshine causing the wintry world to smile. We had proceeded
more than half way to Laurel Hill without event, when,
driving my heavy-shouldered brute at a bank, instead of
lifting up his feet, he thought fit to stumble, fall, and fling
me very comfortably off the mound. I sprang up, neither
hurt nor frightened, shook my habit, tightened my girths,
and mounted again. We set off, much refreshed by this little incident, which occasioned a world of mirth, and many
saucy speeches from my companions.

At Laurel Hill the master of the house came bowing forth
with the utmost courteousness to meet me, expressing his
profound sense of the honour I did him in deigning to in-
hale the air around his abode, and his unspeakable anguish
at having been absent when I had so far condescended before. He was a foreigner, French or Italian, which accounts

for his civility. He had the horses taken to the stable, and their girths slackened.

Dall kept to the heights, and Edward Biddle and I ran, slipped, slid and scrambled down to the water's edge. The river was frozen over, not, however, strongly enough to bear much, and every jutting rock was hung with pure glittering icicles that shone like jewels in the bright sunshine. Far down the river all was still and lonely and bright, yet wintry-looking.

Turning to re-ascend the rocks, I called aloud to Dall, and the distinctest, loudest echo answered me. So perfect was the reflection of the sound, that at first I thought someone was mocking me. I ran up a scale as loud, high and rapid as I could, and from among the sunny fields, a voice repeated the notes as clearly, as rapidly, only more softly, with a distinctness that was startling. I never heard an echo that repeated so much of what was said or sung. I stood in perfect enchantment exercising my voice, and provoking the hidden voice of the air, who answered me with a far off tone, that seemed as though the mocking spirit fled along the hill tops, repeating my notes with a sweet gleeful tone, that filled me with delight.

At length we joined Dall, and walked to the house, where presently appeared the master of the mansion, with cakes, wine, cordial, preserves, or, as Comus has it, "a table covered with all manner of deliciousness". I was at first a little puzzled by the epithet *cordial* applied to three goodly-looking decanters full of rosy and golden liquor, which Edward Biddle informed me is the invariable refreshment presented to visitors of both sexes who ride or drive up to Laurel Hill. To satisfy my curiosity, I put my lips to some of it, which proved to be no other than liqueur, that which sober folks in England take but a thimble full of after dinner, by way of "chasse café", but the drunkenest folk would be ashamed to touch in the morning. It seems otherwise here. The men take brandy in a way that would astound people of any respectability in England, and in this, as well as in other ways, contribute to assist the enervating effects of their climate.

Spirituous liquors are alone the fashion among the numerous frequenters of the gin palaces of Holborn and St. Giles. The fragrant and delicate wines of Burgundy, Bordeaux and the Rhine, are the wines now preferred before all others by persons of refined taste and moderate indulgence. Our gentlemen have learnt to consider hard drinking ungentlemanly. I wish I could say the same of American gentlemen.

Our host waited himself most attentively upon us, and refused all species of remuneration save thanks, which, indeed he said he owed me for so far honouring him as to stuff his cakes and drink his wine. We mounted again, being refreshed, and taking leave of this parcel of innkeepers, continued our ride along the banks of the Schuylkill, until we came to Manayunk, a manufacturing place, where they create cottons. It was getting late, however, and we pushed on to the bridge; but lo! when we reached it, it was under repair and impassable. What was to be done? To turn back was disheartening—to go on for the chance of a bridge was also to run the chance of being utterly benighted in paths we knew nothing of, and on horses which were anything but safe.

However my inclination to the latter course prevailed with my companions, and we pursued a sort of tow-path between the canal and the river. The glimmering daylight was fading fast from the sky, when, from between two beautiful masses of rock, the wooden bridge appeared. On we went over the bridge, and, turning to the left, pursued the river's side—now, close down to its gushing waters, now high above its course, in the woods growing to the very edge of the precipice, and from which descended, at every ten yards, a trickling rill, which, smoothed over by the glassy ice, rendered our horses' footing, particularly in the twilight, very insecure. I pushed on with much care as I could, on Mr. Beckett's tumble-down charger, whose headlong motion kept me in agonies, leaving Edward Biddle to take care of dear Dall, whose bones I feared would ache for this adventure most bitterly. We did not reach Philadelphia till it was perfectly dark.

Tuesday, December 25th, Christmas Day

I WISH myself a merry Christmas, poor child! away from home and friends. After breakfast, drove out shopping with Dall, and bought a rocking horse for Mrs. Dulaney's chicks, whose merry voices I shall miss most horribly by and by. Dragged it in to them in the midst of their dinner. After our dinner went and sat with her till coffee time. Went to the theatre; the house was crammed with men, and very noisy—a Christmas audience. The play was *Macbeth*; I only played so-so.

There is a species of home religion, so to speak, which is kept alive by the gathering together of families at stated periods of joy and festivity, which has a far deeper moral than people imagine. The merry-making at Christmas, the watching out of the old year and in the new, the keeping of birthdays, and the anniversaries of weddings, are things, which, may savour of childishness or superstition, but they tend to promote and keep alive some of the sweetest charities and kindliest sympathies of our poor nature. While we are yet children, those days are set in golden letters in the calendar, long looked forward to, enjoyed with delight, the peculiar seasons of new frocks, new books, new toys, drinking of healths, and being brought into the notice of our elders.

In this country I have been mournfully struck with the absence of anything like this home-clinging. Here are comparatively no observance of tides and times. Christmas day is no religious day, and hardly a holiday with them. New Year's day is perhaps a little, but only a little more so.

Wednesday, December 26th

D R. Hosack called today. I was quite glad to see him. He gave me all the New York news, and brought with him, a gentleman, a friend of his, who nearly made me sick, by very deliberately spitting upon the carpet. Mercy on me! I thought I should have jumped off my chair, I was so disgusted.

Went to the theatre at half past five. The house was very fair, considering the weather, which was very foul. The play—*The School for Scandal.* They none of them knew their parts, or remembered their business—delightful people, indeed! I played only so-so. Pierce Butler supped with us. He is a very gentlemanly, nice person, and I am told is extremely amiable.

Saturday, December 29th

W HEN I came down to breakfast, I found a very pretty diamond ring and some Scotch rhymes from Mr. Maywood, what we call a small return of favours. I wish my hand wasn't so abominably ugly—I hate to put a ring upon it. Pierce Butler called to see if we would ride, but Dall had too much to do—and after sitting pottering for some time,

I sang him the "Messenger Bird", and sent him away. Went out to pay sundry bills and visits. Called at Mr. Sully's, and spent half an hour delightfully in his studio. His picture of my father is very like and very agreable. 'Tis too youthful by a good deal, but the expression of his face is extremely good, and 'tis the likest thing I have seen of him. We had a long discussion about the stage. Now I am a living and breathing witness that a person may be accounted a good actor and to a certain degree deserve that title, without time or pains of any sort being expended upon the acquisition of the reputation. Acting had always appeared to me to be the very lowest of the arts, admitting that it deserves to be classed among them at all, which I am not sure it does. In the first place, it originates nothing; it lacks, therefore, the grand faculty which all other arts possess—creation. An actor is at best but the filler up of the outline designated by another—the expounder, as it were, of things which another has set down. A fine piece of acting is at best, in my opinion, a fine translation.

Art must be to a certain degree enduring. And here it is that the miserable deficiency of acting is most apparent. Where are the labours of Garrick, of Macklin, of Cooke, or Kemble, of Mrs. Siddons? chronicled in the dim memories of some few of their surviving spectators. What have these great actors left either to delight the sense, or elevate the soul, but barren names, unwedded to a single lasting evidence of greatness. If, then, acting be without the creating power, and the enduring property, which are at once the highest faculty of art, and its most beneficial purpose, what becomes of it when ranked with efforts displaying both in the highest degree. To me it seems no art, but merely a highly interesting and exciting amusement, and I think man may as well, much better perhaps, spend three hours in a theatre, then in a billiard or bar-room—and this is the extent of my approbation and admiration of my art.

Monday, December 31st

THE river being yet open thank heaven, we arose at half past four o'clock. Dressed and came down, and Dall and I were bundled into a coach, and rumbled and tumbled over the stones, through the darkness down to the steamboat. Pierce Butler was waiting for us, and convoyed us safely to the cabin, where I laid myself down, and slept till breakfast time. My father, Mr. Bancroft, and Baron Hackelberg sat themselves down to breakfast, leaving Dall and I entirely to the charge and care of Pierce Butler, who fulfilled his trust with infinite zeal. 'Tis curious, there was a man on board whom I have seen every time I have been going to or from New York to Philadelphia, whose appearance was in itself very remarkable, and the subsequent account I received of him, perhaps increased the sort of impression it made upon me. He was a man of about thirty to thirty five, I guess, standing about five feet ten, with a great appearance of strength and activity. His face was that of a foreigner, the features were remarkably well cut, and the piercing black eyes, dark hair and brown complexion, gave a Spanish character to his countenance. There was a sort of familiar would-be gentlemanly manner in his deportment and address, and a species of slang gentility in his carriage and conversation, that gave me a curiosity to ascertain what on earth he could be. After breakfast, walked up and down the deck with Pierce Butler; Mr. Staley was on board. I am happy to hear he is thriving; I love all my fellow passengers, and when I see one of them my heart warms toward them, as to a bit of the dear old land left behind. After about an hour's steaming, we disembarked to cross

126

the narrow neck of land which divides the Delaware from the Chesapeake. Here we got into a coach holding some twelve of us, to be conveyed over the rail-road by one of Stephenson's engines. Neither the road nor the conveyances are comparable to those of the Liverpool and Manchester rail-way. Instead of those luxurious and roomy coaches, which form the merit of the Liverpool train, we were squeezy and uncomfortable to a degree.

The distance from the Delaware to Frenchtown, on the Elk, where we were again to take to the water, is about sixteen miles, which we did in an hour. The first part of the road lies in Delaware, the latter in Maryland. The Elk, which in this world of huge waters is considered but a paltry ditch, but which in our country would be thought a very decent-sized river, was, a few days ago, frozen up, thereby putting a stop to the steamboat travelling. But fortunately for us it was open today, and presently we beheld the steamboat coming puffing up to take us from the pier. This boat—the *Charles Carroll*—is one of the finest they have. It is a beautiful vessel, roomy and comfortable in its arrangements. I went below for a few moments, but found, as usual, the atmosphere of the cabin perfectly intolerable. The ladies' cabin, in winter, on board one of these large steamers, is a right curious sight. 'Tis generally crammed to suffocation with women, strewn in every direction. The greater number cuddle round a stove, the heat of which would alone make the atmosphere unbreathable. Others sit lazily in a sort of rocking-chair, which is found wherever Americans sit down, and others manage again, even upon fresh water, to be very sick.

At dinner, Mr. and Mrs. Bancroft took charge of Dall and me. The strange dark man was sitting opposite us, and discoursing away to his neighbours in a strain and tone in which shrewdness and swagger, vulgarity and a sort of braggart gallantry were curiously jumbled. From his conversation it was evident he was a sea-faring man. He spoke of having been a midshipman aboard an American frigate. When dinner was over, I pointed out this strange man to my father, asking him if he had any idea who he was. "I am told," was his reply, "that he has just returned from New York, where he has been tried for piracy". This accounted for everything—dare-devil look and language, seafaring adventure and superstitious creed. It is a pleasant mode of travelling that throws one into contact with such company.

Touching pirates, Baltimore, I was told, is famous for them. They have small schooners there of a particularly light build and raking masts, which are the prettiest craft to look at and the swiftest that sail the sea. The Baltimore clippers are proverbial for their elegance and fleetness—they are like greyhounds on the water. They were frequently owned by gentlemen of an ambiguous character, something between pirate, smuggler and wrecker. Their trade is chiefly with and about the West Indian islands. I looked at my Spanish friend with redoubled curiosity—he was the very man for a pirate.

We reached Baltimore at about half past four. The Chesapeake Bay, like the Delaware river, appeared to me admirable only as an immense sheet of water. At some parts that we passed, it was six, at others, ten, and at others thirteen miles across. The day was more lovely than a fine day in early September in England, bright, soft and sunny, with in the sky the delicate colour one sees in Sèvres porcelain. As we entered the Patapsco, and neared Baltimore, North Point and Fort M'Henry were pointed out to me. My spirits always sink when I come to a strange place, and as we came alongside the wharf, under the dingy-looking red warehouses, between which the water ran in narrow dark canals, I felt terribly gloomy. We drove up to Barnham's, the best house in town, and having found out where to lay my head, I had my fill of crying. After dinner went and lay down again, and slept profoundly till nine o'clock.

XIV

Impressions of the theatre and the town of Baltimore—Service in a Catholic church—Disastrous performance of Romeo and Juliet*— Journey to Washington—Visit to the Capitol—Large and small theatres—Real feeling in acting—Gossip about Fanny*

Baltimore, Tuesday, January 1st, 1833

BEGAN writing my journal. 'Twas not until dating it that I discovered it was New Year's day. When I did so and looked at my strange surroundings, at the gloomy wintry sky, I could not refrain from crying bitterly. In spite of the pouring rain, my father, who wished to ascertain the truth of the reports of the state of the theatre, set forward thither with me. We found a very large handsome house, larger, I think, than the Park, but dirty, dilapidated, and looking as if there had been eleven executions in it that morning. No actors, hardly any scenes, in short, such a state of things that rendered it totally impossible for us to think of acting there.

Came home and later the afternoon cleared up and became soft and sunny. My father insisted on my taking a walk so I bonneted and set out with him. What I saw of the town appeared to me extremely like the outskirts of Birmingham or Manchester. Bright brick-red houses, in rows of three to five, with interesting gaps of gravel pits, patches of meadow and open spaces between, which give it an untidy straggling appearance. They are building in every direction, however, and in less than two years these little pauses being filled up, Baltimore will be a very considerable place, for it covers, in its present state, a large extent of ground, and contains a vast population.

Immediately after dinner, our host made his entrance with a pianoforte. I had suggested to Mr. Staley that I should be glad to have one, and here it came. I had asked him to return in the evening, and was glad of the piano, as it helps the time away. At six o'clock the managers of the Holliday Street theatre made their appearance, and my father entered into arrangements with them. During which, I sat at a tremendously high window, looking at the beautiful skies and radiant moon, and listening to a tolerable band playing sundry of Rossini's airs.

When these men had departed, Mr. Staley came in, and I sang and made him sing till teatime. After that he entertained us with a very long, but not very clear account of the various processes of making, polishing etc., steel, as practised in his manufactory. His account of the hard dealings with the proper manufacturers was dreadful, and he himself spoke with horror of it, saying, "Oh they are so miserably ground, poor wretches, they cannot be said to live, they barely exist". When I remonstrated with him upon the wickedness of such proceedings, he replied, "We are compelled to do it in self-defence. If we did not use the same means as other manufacturers, we should presently be undersold".

I at length spoke, and burst into an eloquent lamentation on the folly and misery of which the world was guilty in following this base worship. But when I said that I was convinced that happiness might and did exist most blessedly upon half the means which men spend their lives scraping together, my father laughed, and said that I was the last person in the world who could live on little, or be content with the mediocrity I vaunted. I looked at my satin gown and held my tongue, but still I was not convinced. We returned to our music till ten o'clock, then we had some supper, and after which we drank a happy new year to England—poor old England, God bless it!

Sunday, January 6th, 1833

AT about half past ten Mr. Staley called for us, and we walked up to the cathedral, which is a large unfinished stone building, standing on the brow of a hill, and where there are already some very nice-looking houses. The interior of the church is large and handsome, and has more the look of a church than anything I have been inside in this country yet. 'Tis full eight years since I was in a Catholic church, and the sensation with which I approached the high altar, with its golden crucifix, its marble entablatures and its glimmering starry lights, savoured as much of sadness as of devotion. I have not been in a Catholic place of worship since I was at school. How well I remember the beautiful music of the military mass, the processions and pageants of the feast days at high mass, and the evening service. They sang that exquisitely mournful and beautiful 'et incarnatus est' of Haydn's, which made my blood run cold. One thing disgusted me dreadfully, though the priests who were officiating never passed or approached the altar without bending the knee to it, they kept spitting all over the carpet that surrounded and covered the steps to it, interrupting themselves in the middle of the service to do so, without the slightest hesitation. We had a very indifferent sermon—the service was of course in Latin. Was introduced to several people coming out of church. A little way beyond the cathedral stands Washington's monument, which, together with a smaller one erected at the head of our street to the memory of the North Point heroes, has given Baltimore the appelation of the monumental city.

At eight o'clock we went to Mrs. Caton's. They are all in deep mourning, and the circle was very small. They are most agreeable pleasant people, with a peculiar gentleness of manner. Their conversation appeared to me to be totally divested of the disagreeable accent which seems almost universal in this country. Mrs. Caton talked to me about my aunt Whitelock, and what a charming actress she was, and what an enchanting thrilling voice she had. I spent a delightful evening. Before we went away, Mr. Caton showed us a very good likeness of the Duke of Wellington. 'Twas very like him, though many years younger.

Mrs. Caton amused me very much by her account of the slaves on their estates, whom, she said, she found the best and most faithful servants in the world. Being born upon the land, there exists among them something of the old spirit of clanship, and "our house", "our family", are the terms by which they designate their owners. In the south there are no servants but blacks, for the greater proportion of domestics being slaves, all species of servitude whatever is looked upon as a degradation, and the slaves themselves entertain the most highest contempt for white servants, whom they designate as "poor white trash".

Monday, January 7th, 1833

AT half past five took coffee, and off to the theatre. The play was *Romeo and Juliet*—the house was extremely full, they are a delightful audience. My Romeo had gotten on a pair of trunk breeches, that looked as if he had borrowed them from some worthy Dutchman of a hundred years ago. They were of a most unhappy choice of colours—dull, heavy-looking blue cloth, and offensive crimson satin, all be-puckered, and be-puffed, till the young man looked like a magical figure growing out of a monstrous, strange-looking melon, beneath which descended his unfortunate legs, thrust into a pair of red slippers. The play went off pretty smoothly, except that they broke one man's collar bone, and nearly dislocated a woman's shoulder by throwing the scenery about. My bed was not made in time, and when the scene drew, half a dozen carpenters were discovered smoothing down my pillows and adjusting my draperies. The last scene is too good not to be given verbatim.

> Romeo: Rise, rise my Juliet,
> And from this cave of death, this
>   house of horror,
> Quick let me snatch thee to thy
>   Romeo's arms.

Here he pounced upon me, plucked me up in his arms like an uncomfortable bundle, and staggered down the stage with me.

> Juliet (*aside*): Oh, you've got me up horridly! that'll
>   never do—let me down, pray let
>   me down!
> Romeo: There, breathe a vital spirit on thy
>   lips,
> And call thee back, my soul, to life
>   and love!
> Juliet (*aside*): Pray put me down; you'll certainly
>   throw me down if you don't set me
>   on the ground directly.

In the midst of "cruel, cursed fate", his dagger fell out of his dress. I embracing him tenderly, crammed it back again, because I knew I should want it at the end.

> Romeo: Tear not our heart—strings thus!
> They crack! they break! Juliet! Juliet!
>   (dies)

Juliet (*to corpse*): Am I smothering you?

Corpse (*to Juliet*): Not at all; could you be so kind please, as to put my wig on again for me?—it has fallen off.

Juliet (*to corpse*): I'm afraid I can't, but I'll throw my muslin veil over it. You've broken the phial, haven't you? (Corpse nodded)

Juliet (*to corpse*): Where's your dagger?

Corpse (*to Juliet*): 'Pon my soul, I don't know.

Sunday, January 13th

BY half past ten we were packed into what in this country is termed an "exclusive extra", i.e. a stage coach to ourselves, and progressing towards Washington. The coach was comfortable enough, and the country, for the first twelve or fourteen miles, was by no means so dreary or desolate as I had been led to expect. There was a considerable variety in its outline, and the quantity of cedar thickets scattered over it took away from the comfortless, threadbare look of wintry woods. The soil, the banks by the roadside, and broken ridges of ravines and water-courses, attracted my attention by the variety and vividness of their colours. The brightest red and yellow, and then again pale green, and rich, warm gravel colour.

The waters were all fast frozen up, and one or two little pools, all curdled with ice, looked like onyx set in gold. As for the road, we had been assured it was exceedingly good, but mercy on us! I can't think of it without aching. Here we went up, up, up, and there we went down, down, down—now I was in my father's lap, and now I was half out of the window. The utter impossibility of holding oneself in any position for two minutes, is absolutely ridiculous. Sometimes we laughed, and at other times we groaned at our helpless and hopeless condition. But at last we arrived, with no bones broken, at about three o'clock, at the capital and seat of government of the United States.

Upon the height immediately above the city, is situated the Capitol, a very handsome building, of which the Americans are not a little proud. But it seems placed there by mistake, so little do the miserable, untidy hovels above, and the scattered, unfinished red-brick town below, accord with its patrician marble, and high-sounding title. We drove to Gadsby's, which is an inn like a little town, with more wooden galleries, flights of steps, passages, doorways, exists and entrances, than any building I ever saw. We had not been arrived a quarter of an hour, when in walked Mr. Bancroft, the English chargé d'affaires, and Captain Byam Martin, and presently Mr. Pitt Adams, attaché to the British Legation. They sat for some time, discussing, laughing, quizzing and being funny, and then departed. Captain Martin was telling a story about a man somewhere up in the lost lands, who was called Philemon, and whose three sons were "paganed" (christened, I suppose one can't say) Romulus, Remus, and Tiberius. I thought this was too good to be true, and Dall and I laughed over it at dinner, agreed that we wished something of the sort had happened to us. "Some bread, waiter; what is your name?" "Horatius!", was the reply, which sent Dall and me into fits.

Monday, January 14th

WHEN I came into breakfast, I found Mr. Everett there, whom I like mainly. While he was here, Washington Irving came in. I gave him a most tremendous grasp of the hand—it was like seeing a bit of old England to see him. He said to me, "Oh how strange it is to see you here", which caused my eyes to fill with tears. They had hardly been seated, when in rushed a boy to call us to rehearsal. I was as vexed as might be. They all departed, Washington Irving faithfully promising to come again, and have a long talk about the old country, we then set forth to rehearsal. The theatre is the tiniest little box that ever was seen—not much bigger I verily think, then the baby's play-house at Versailles. When I came to perceive who the company were, and that sundry of our Baltimore comrades were come on hither, I begged to be excused from rehearsing, as they had all done their parts but a few days before with me.

At about two o'clock, Mr. Bancroft came to take us to the Capitol. Mr. Everett was in the drawing room. He had just seen the President, and it seems, that far from coming to any accommodation with the South Carolinians, there is an immediate probability of their coming to blows. They say, the old general is longing for a fight, and most assuredly, to fight would be better, than to give in. To yield, would be virtually to admit the right of every individual state to dictate to the whole government.

We walked up to the Capitol. The day was most beautifully bright and sunny, and the mass of white buildings, with its terraces and columns, stood out in fine relief against the cloudless blue sky. We went first into the senate, or upper house, because Webster was speaking, whom I especially wished to hear. The room itself is neither large nor lofty, the senators sit in two semi-circular rows, turned towards the president, in comfortable arm-chairs. On the same ground, and literally sitting among the senators, were a whole regiment of ladies, whispering, talking, laughing, and fidgeting. A gallery, level with the floor, and only divided by a low partition from the main room, ran round the apartment. This too, was filled with pink, blue and yellow bonnets, and every now and then, while the business of the house was going on, and Webster speaking, a tremendous bustle and waving of feathers and rustling of silks would be heard, and in came streaming a reinforcement of political beauties, and then would commence a jumping up, a sitting down, a squeezing through a how-d'ye-doing, and a shaking of hands. The senators would turn round, even Webster would hestitate as if bothered by the row, and, in short, the whole thing was more irregular and unbusinesslike than anyone could have imagined. Webster's face is very remarkable, particularly the forehead and eyes. The former projects singularly, absolutely overhanging the latter, which have a very melancholy and occasionally rather wild expression. The subject upon which he was speaking was not one of particular interest—an estimate of the amount of French spoliations, by cruisers and privateers, upon American commerce. The heat of the room was intolerable, and after sitting till I was nearly suffocated, we adjourned to the House of Representatives.

On our way thither, we crossed a very beautiful circular vestibule, which holds the centre of the building. It was adorned with sundry memorable passages in American history done into pictures, by Colonel Trumbell. In the House of Representatives we were told that we should hear nothing of interest, so turned off, under Mr. Everett's escort, to the library, which is a comfortable well-sized room. We looked over Audubon's Ornithology, a beautiful work, and saw a man sitting with his feet on a table, reading, which is an American fashion. Met half the New York world there.

After we had stayed there some time, we went into the House of Representatives. The room itself is lofty and large and very handsome, but extremely ill-constructed for the voice, which is completely lost among the columns, and only reaches the gallery, where listeners are admitted, in indistinct and very unedifying murmurs. The members not infrequently sit with their feet upon their desks. We walked out upon the terrace, and looked at the view of the Potomac, and the town, which, in spite of the enlivening effect of an almost summer's sky, looked dreary and desolate in the extreme. We then returned home.

At half past five we went to the theatre. We were a long time before we could discover, among the intricate, dark, little passages, our own private entrance, and were as nearly as possible carried into the pit by a sudden rush of spectators making their way thither. I wish we had been; I think I should like to have seen myself. The theatre is absolutely like a doll's play-house. It was completely crammed with people. I played ill—I cannot act tragedy within half a yard of people in the boxes. By the bye, a theatre may very easily be too small for tragedies which is admirably adapted for comedies. In the latter species of dramatic representations, the incidents, characters, manners and dresses, are for the most part, modern—such as we meet with, or can easily imagine in our own drawing-rooms, and among our own society. There is little if any exaggeration of colouring necessary, and no great exertion of fancy needful either in the actor or audience in executing or witnessing such a performance. On the contrary, comedy generally embodying the manners, tone and spirit of the higher classes of society, the smaller the space in which such personifications take place, the less danger there is of the actor's departing from that natural, quiet and refined deportment and delivery, which are, in the present day, the general characteristics of polished society.

'Tis otherwise with tragic representations. They are unnatural, not positively, but comparatively unnatural. The incidents are, for the most part, strange, startling, unusual. They are events which come within the probabilities of few of us, and this renders necessary a degree of excitement and elevation in the mind of the spectator.

Again, the scene of a comedy is generally a drawing room, and the smaller the stage, the greater the possibility of rendering it absolutely like what we have all seen, and are daily in the habit of seeing. But to represent groves, mountains, or lakes, or the dwellings of the kings of the earth, satisfactorily in the spectator's mind, there must be a certain distance observed. In closer contact with such scenes, the near and absolute detail of paint, canvas and gilding is obtruded in a manner that destroys all illusion. The same thing applies to dress. Foil, stone, paste and coloured glass, have been manufactured into toys, which, with the help of distance, may be admitted as representing the splendours of Eastern costume, or even the glittering trappings of those gaudy little superhumans, the fairies. But nearness utterly dissolves the spell. So much for little theatres.

Mr. Staley came in after the play. He told us that as he was coming out of the theatre a Kentuckian accosted him with—"Well, what do you think of that 'ere gal?". "Oh", hesitatingly replied Staley, "I don't quite know"—"Well", retorted the questioner, "any how, I guess she's o' some account".

Tuesday, January 15th

AT eleven o'clock Mr. Everett called and we went with him to see the original of the Declaration of Independence, also, a few medals, for the most part modern ones, and neither of much beauty or curiosity. Afterwards we went to the War Office, where we saw sundry Indian properties—bows and arrows, canoes, smoking pipes, and the pictures of a great many savage chiefs, and one or two of Indian women. The latter were rather pretty, but the men were not any of them handsome. Scorn round the mouth, and cunning in the eyes seemed to be the general characteristic of all the faces.

After we had done seeing what was to be seen, we went on to the President's house, which is a comfortless, handsome-looking building, with a withered grass-plot enclosed in wooden palings in front, and a desolate reach of uncultivated ground down to the river behind. Mr. Everett gave us a most entertaining account of the levées, or rather public days, at the president's house. Every human being has the right to present himself there. The consequence is, that great numbers of the very commonest sort of people used to rush in, and follow the servants who carried refreshments, seizing upon whatever they could get, and staring and pushing about, to the great discomforture of the more respectable and well-behaved part of the assembly. Indeed, the nuisance became so great, that they discontinued the estables, and in great measure got rid of the crowd.

Wednesday, January 16th

AT half past twelve Mr. Everett came to ride with me. The horse he had gotten for me was base, but never mind, the day was exquisitely mild and bright—the sort of early spring-feeling day, when in England the bright gold, and pale delicate violet of the crocus buds begin to break the rich, dark mould, and the fragrant gummy leaves of the lilac bushes open their soft brown folds. We had a very pleasant ride through some pretty woodlands on the opposite side of the river. At half past five went to the theatre. The play was *The Hunchback*—the house was crowded. Mr. Everett and Washington Irving came in after the play. We had a discussion as to how far real feeling enters into our scenic performances. 'Tis hard to say; the general question it would be impossible to answer, for acting is altogether a monstrous anomaly. John Kemble and Mrs. Siddons were always in earnest in what they were about; Miss O'Neill used to cry bitterly in all her tragedy parts; whilst Garrick could be making faces and playing tricks in the middle of his finest points, and Kean would talk gibberish while the people were in an uproar of applause at his. In my own individual instance, I know that sometimes I could turn every word I am saying into burlesque, (*never* Shakespeare, by the bye), and at others my heart aches, and I cry real, bitter, warm tears, as earnestly as if I was in earnest.

Thursday, January 17th

SAT writing journal till twelve o'clock, when we went to Mr. Bancroft's, and thence proceeded to the Presidency to be presented in due form. His excellency Andrew Jackson is very tall and thin, but erect and dignified in his carriage—a good specimen of a fine old well-battered soldier. His hair is very thick and grey, his manners are perfectly simple and quiet, therefore, very good. So are those of his niece, Mrs. Everett, who is a very pretty person, and lady of the house, Mrs. Jackson having been dead some time. He talked about South Carolina, and entered his protest against scribbling ladies, assuring us that the whole of the present southern disturbances had their origin in no larger a source than the nib of the pen of a lady. If this be true, the lady must have scribbled to some purpose. We sat a little while and afterwards adjourned to Mr. Adam's house.

At about one o'clock Mr. Everett called for me. On going to the door I found him and his horse, and a strange tall grey horse for me, and a young gentleman, of the name of Fulton, to whom I understood it belonged, and whom Mr. Everett introduced to me as anxious to join our party. I was a little startled at this, as I did not think that Mr. Everett ought to have brought anybody to ride with me without my leave. However, as I was riding his horse, I was just as well pleased that he was by, for I don't like having the responsibility of such valuable property as a private gentleman's horse to take care of. I told him this, alleging it as a reason for my preferring to ride an indifferent hack horse, about which I had no such anxiety. He replied that I need have none about his. I told him laughingly that I would give him two dollars for the hire of it, and then I should feel happy, all of which nonsense passes as nonsense should, without a comment.

We rode till half past three. The horse I was upon, Mr. Fulton assured me, was an English one, but he had been long enough in this world to learn racking, and forget every other more Christian pace—he tired me dreadfully.

After dinner wrote journal till time to go to the theatre. The play was *The School for Scandal,* in the fourth act of which Joseph Surface assured me that I was a *plethora!* Mr. Everett came in and supped with us after the play. He gave us a very interesting account of a school that had been attempted to be formed in Massachusetts, for the purpose of educating young men of the savage tribes, who were willing to become Christian and receive instruction. It was obliged, however, to be given up, in consequence of several of them having fallen in love with and married American girls, whom they took away into the woods, many of them after they were there returning to their savage ways of living, which must have placed their wretched Christian wives in a horrible situation.

Friday, January 18th

AFTER dinner wrote journal, and at half past five went to the theatre. The play was *The Hunchback*, and the house was very good. I wonder if anybody on earth can form the slightest idea of the interior of this wretched little theatre. 'Tis the smallest I was ever in. The proprietors are poor, the actors poorer. The grotesque mixture of misery, vulgarity, stage-finery and real raggedness, is beyond everything strange, sad and revolting—it reminds me constantly of some of Hogarth's pictures.

Saturday, January 19th

AFTER breakfast went to rehearsal, and then walked with my father to see a very pretty model of what is to be the town-hall. It never will be, for the corporation are as poor as *Job's kittens* (Americanism, communicated by Captain Martin), and the City of Washington itself is only kept alive by Congress. Talking of Washington—'tis the strangest thing by way of a town that can be imagined. It is laid out to cover, I should think, some ten miles square, but the houses are here, there, and nowhere. The streets, not properly so-called, are roads, crooked or straight, where buildings are *intended* to be. Every now and then an interesting gap of a quarter of a mile occurs between those houses that *are* built. In the midst of the town you can't help feeling that you are in the country, and between wooden palings, with nothing to be seen on either side but cedar bushes and sand, you are informed you are in the midst of the town. Washington altogether struck me as a rambling red-brick image of futurity, where nothing *is*, but all things *are to be*.

Directly after dinner, I set out to pay sundry calls. The day had been heavenly bright, warm and balmy. The evening was beautifully soft and as I drove over hill and dale, through the city of Washington, paying my calls, the stars came out one after the other in the still sky. One of my calls lay nearly three miles out of town, so that I was not back till six o'clock. As I came rushing along the corridor, I met Dall coming to meet me, with an air of mingled horror and satisfaction. "Oh, here you are! here is coffee and Mr. Featherstone waiting for you!" I went into the room and found a goodly looking personage, old enough to know better, sitting with my father, who appeared amazingly disturbed, holding an open letter in his hand. He exclaimed the moment I came in, "There, sir, there is the young lady to speak for herself". I courtesied, and sat down, "Fanny", quoth my father, "something particularly disagreeable has occurred. Pray, can you call to mind anything you said during the course of your Thursday's ride, which was likely to be offensive to Mr. Fulton or anything abusive of this country?" I untied my bonnet, and replied that I did not at that moment recollect a word I had said during my whole ride, and should certainly not give myself any trouble to do so. "Now, my dear", said my father, his eyes flashing with indignation, "don't put yourself into a passion; compose yourself and recollect. Here is a letter I have just received". He proceeded to read it, and the contents were to this effect—that during my ride with Mr. Fulton, I had said that I did not choose to ride an American gentleman's horse, and had offered him two dollars for the hire of his. That moreover I had spoken most derogatorily of America and Americans, in consequence of which, if my father did not give some explanation, or make some apology to the public, I should certainly be hissed off the stage as soon as I appeared on it that evening. This was pleasant!

I stated the conversation as it has passed, adding, that liberty of opinion, and liberty of speech were alike rights that belonged to everyone, and that, with a due regard to good breeding and good feeling, they were rights which nobody ought, and which I never would forgo. Mr. Featherstone opened his eyes, and said, "Not less than *fifty* members of Congress have already mentioned the matter to me". Fifty old gossiping women! why the whole thing is for all the world like a village tattle in England, among half a dozen old wives round their tea-pots. All Washington was in dismay, and my evil deeds and evil words were the town talk. It gave me at the time, a dreadful side-ache and nervous cough.

I went to the theatre, dressed and came on the stage in the full expectation of being hissed off it. A pleasant sensation, very, and it made my heart full of bitterness to think I should stand—as no woman ought to stand—the mark of public insult. However, no such thing occurred—I went on and came off without any such trial of my courage. But I had been so much annoyed, that I passed the intervals between my scenes in crying—which of course added greatly to the mirth and spirit of my performance of Beatrice. In the middle of the play, Mr. Adams and Captain Martin came behind the scenes, and I *was* glad to see Englishmen. Their compassionate sympathies for my wrongs, and tender fears lest I should catch cold behind those horrid scenes, very nearly set me off crying again. But I was ashamed to cry before them, so tried to keep my heart-swellings down.

Wednesday, January 30th, Philadelphia

WENT to the theatre at half past five. It poured with rain, in spite of which the house was very good— the play was *Fazio*. When I came on in my fine dress, at the beginning of the second act, the people hailed me with such a tremendous burst of applause and prolonged it so much, that I was greatly puzzled to imagine what on earth possessed them. I concluded they were rather pleased with my dress. However they ceased at last, and I thought no more about it. Towards the time for the beginning of the third act, as I was sitting in my dressing-room, Dall suddenly exclaimed, "Hark! what is that?"—she opened the door and we heard a tremendous noise of shouts and applause. "They are waiting for you, certainly", said Dall. She ran out, and returned saying, "The stage is certainly waiting for you, Fanny, for the curtain is up". I rushed out of the room, but on opening the door leading to the stage, I distinctly heard my father's voice addressing the audience. On inquiry I found that at the beginning of the play a number of handbills had been thrown into the pit, professing to quote my conversation with Mr. Fulton in Washington, and calling upon the people to resent my conduct in the grossest and most vulgar of terms. This precious document had, it seems, been brought round by somebody to my father, who immediately went on with it in his hand, and assured the audience that the whole thing was a falsehood. I was crying dreadfully with fright and indignation. How I wished I was a caterpillar under a green gooseberry bush!

Oh, how I did wince to think of going on again after this scene, though the feeling of the audience was most evident. All the applause I had fancied they had bestowed upon my dress, was, in fact, an unsolicited testimony of their disbelief in the accusation brought against me. They received my father's words with acclamations, and when the curtain drew up, and I was discovered, the pit rose and waved their hats, and the applause was tremendous.

Saturday, February 2nd, 1833

AFTER breakfast Pierce Butler called to see how I did
after my walk; he sat for some time. At twelve went
out paying calls, and then spent a delightful hour with Mr.
Sully and his family. He is a most agreeable person, but he
thinks too well of acting. After dinner went to Mrs. Dulaney's room, and remained there till time to go to the theatre. The play was *The Gamester;* it was my benefit, and I
am afraid the good folks who addressed their amiable placard to the public will have been rather ill satisfied with their
suggestion about my benefit. The house was literally
crammed, in consequence of that very circumstance—
crammed is the word. When the curtain drew up, they applauded me without end, and I courtesied as profoundly as
I was able. Indeed, I am extremely obliged to this same excellent public for they have testified most satisfactorily in
every way, the kindest possible feeling for me, and the most
entire faith in my good behaviour. I did not play well—my
voice was so dreadfully affected by my cough.

DINED at three. After dinner, Mrs. Dulaney came into our room where I sang and played till time to go to the theatre. The play was *The Merchant of Venice* and Katharine and Petruchio for the farce—my father's benefit. The house was crammed from floor to ceiling as full as it could hold; so much for the success of the handbills. Indeed, as somebody suggested, I think if we could find the author of that placard, we are bound to give him a handsome reward, for he has certainly given us two of the finest benefits that were ever seen. At the end, the people shouted and shrieked for us. My father went on and made them a speech, and I went and made them a courtesy. Certainly they do deserve the civilest of speeches and lowest of courtesies from us, for they have behaved most kindly and courteously to us, and for mine own part, I love the whole city of Philadelphia from this time forth for ever more. Mr. Pierce Butler came round to the stage door to bid us good-night, and as we drove off, a whole parcel of people who had gathered round the door to see us depart, set up a universal hurrah! How strange a thing it is, that popular shout!

Wednesday, February 13th, New York

AFTER dinner, Grant Thorburn came in. He sat himself down, and presently was overhead with reminiscences. His account of Tom Paine's escape from the Conciergerie, on the eve of being guillotined, was extremely interesting. His own introduction to, and subsequent acquaintance with that worthy, was equally so, and his summing up was highly characteristic. "I tell ye, madam, the saving of that man's life was an especial providence. If Paine had been guillotined, madam, he would have been a martyr, and his works would have had ten times the power of evil they had before. But he lived to be a miserable, unthrifty sot, and died neglected and despised by all reputable and respectable individuals, and I say again, it was a manifest providence that he did so."

Monday, February 18th

AFTER breakfast went to rehearsal. My father is extremely unwell; I scarce think he will be able to get through his part tonight. At half past five went to the theatre. The play was Macbeth for my benefit—the house was very full and I played very ill. My father was dreadfully exhausted by his work. I had an interesting discussion with Mr. Ogden Hoffman about the costume and acting of the witches in this awful play. I should like to see them acted and dressed a little more like what they should be, than they generally are. It has always been customary—heaven knows why—to make low comedians act the witches, and to dress them like old fish women. Instead of the wild unearthly appearance which Banquo describes, we have three jolly-faced fellows—whom we are accustomed to laugh at, night after night, in every farce of the stage—with as due a proportion of petticoats as any woman, letting alone a witch, might desire, jocose red faces, peaked hat and broomsticks. If I had the casting of Macbeth, I would give the witches to the first melodramatic actors on the stage— such men as T. P. Cooke, and O. Smith, who understand all that belongs to picturesque devilry to perfection. And give them such dresses, as, without ceasing to be grotesque, should be a little more fanciful, and less ridiculous than the established livery; something that would accord better with the blasted heath, the dark, fungus-grown wood, the desolate misty hill-side, and the flickering light of the cauldron cave.

AFTER breakfast Mr. Staley and Mr. Bell came, and Mr. Staley gave me the words and tune of a bewitching old English ballad. Mr. Sedgwick called and sat some time with me; I like him mainly, he's very pleasant and clever. After dinner came to my room, sang over Mr. Staley's ballad, and amused myself writing one of my own. At half past five, took coffee and off to the theatre. The house was very full—the play, *The Stranger.* I didn't play well. I'd on a gown that did not fit me, to which species of accident our art is marvellously subservient. A tight armhole shall mar the grandest passage in Queen Constance, and too long or too short a skirt keep one's heart cold in the balcony scene in Juliet. Came home, supped, and finished marking *A Winter's Tale.* What a dense fool that fat old Johnson must have been in matters of poetry! his notes upon Shakespeare make one swear, and his summing up of *The Winter's Tale* is worthy of a newspaper critic of the present day—in spirit, I mean, not language, Johnson always wrote good English. What dry and sapless and dusty earth his soul must have been made of, poor fat man!

AT two, Pierce Butler and the horses were waiting for me. We mounted and rode down to the Hoboken ferry, where we crossed. The day was like an early day in spring in England, a day when the almond trees would all have been in flower, the hawthorn hedges putting forth their tender and green and brown shoots, and the primroses gemming the mossy roots of the trees by the water-courses. The spring is backwarder here a good deal than with us— but to be sure, it is sudden compared with ours. I do not like this. I like to linger over the sweet hourly and daily fulfilment of hope, which the slow progress of vegetation in my own dear country allows one full enjoyment.

The melted snows had made the roads almost impassable, however, the day was delightfully mild and sunny, and therefore we did not get chilled by the very temperate rate at which we were obliged to proceed. We turned off to look at the Turtle Pavilion, and pursuing the water's edge, got up upon a species of high dyke between some marshes that open into the river. Our path was presently intercepted by a stile, and as the horses were not quite of the sort one could have a leap with, Pierce Butler got off and endeavoured to lead his charger round the edge of the steep bank, but the brute refused that road, and we were forced to turn back. After floundering about over some of the roughest worst ground imaginable, we went out of the Hoboken domain at the gate where we entered, and pursued that beautiful road overlooking the Hudson, under that fine range of cliffs which are the first idea, as it were, of the Palisadoes. We took the lower road down to the glen below Weehawk. The sun shone gloriously. The little stream that owns this narrow glade, was singing and dancing along its beautiful domain with a sweet gleesome voice.

We left the muddy road, and turned our horses into the stream, but its bed was very stoney and uneven and we were obliged to turn out of it again.

We rode up to the house on the height. The house itself is too unsheltered for comfort, but the view from its site is beautiful, and we had it in perfection today. Standing at an elevation of more than a hundred feet from the river, we looked down on its magnificent, broad, silvery avenue, to the narrows—that rocky gate that opens towards my home. New York lay bright and distinct on the opposite shore, glittering like a heap of toys in the sunny distance. The water towards Sandy Hook was studded with sails, and far up on the other side the river rolled away among shores that, even in this wintry time of bare trees and barren earth, looked gay and lovely in the sunshine. We turned down again, but after crossing the bridge over the pretty brook, we took an upper path, and riding through some leafless, warm, and sunny woodlands, joined the road that leads to the Weehawken height, and so returned to New York.

Saturday, April 13th, 1833

A T a quarter after four drove down to the boat. Mr. Staley was waiting to see us off, and Mr. Pierce Butler presently made his appearance to see us on. Owing to yesterday's boat not having sailed, it was crowded today, and proceeded at a much slower rate than common. At a few minutes after five the huge brazen bell on deck began to toll, the mingled crowd jostled and pushed, the loiterers on shore rushed on board, the bidders-farewell on board rushed on shore. Dall and I took a quiet sunny stand away from all the confusion, and watched, from our floating palace, New York glide away like a glittering dream before us. A floating palace indeed it was, in size and magnificence. I never saw anything to compare with the beauty and comfort and largeness of all its accommodations. Our Scotch steam-boat, the *United Kingdom,* is a cockboat to it, and even the splendid Hudson boat, the *North America,* is far inferior to it in every respect, except, I believe, swiftness—but then these Boston boats have sometimes very heavy seas to go through.

Besides the ladies' cabin, this boat is furnished with half a dozen state rooms, taken from the upper deck, an inexpressible luxury. Into one of these our night-bags were conveyed, and we returned to the deck to watch the sun down. A strong and piercing wind blew over the waters and almost cut me in half as I stood watching the shores, which I did not want to lose by going in. However, I might have done so and lost but little, for after passing Hell-gate, where the rocks in the river and the banks have rather a picturesque appearance, there was neither form nor comeliness in the flat, wearisome land to either side.

At about eight we were summoned to tea, which was a compound meal of tea and supper. The company was so numerous that they were obliged to lay the table twice. We waited till the crowd had devoured their feed, and had ours in peace and quiet. An excellent man, by name, Captain Neill, an officer in the American army, made himself known to me, considering, as he afterwards told me, his commission to be a sufficient right of introduction to anybody. He was a native of Boston, and was returning to it after an absence of fourteen years.

Sunday, April 14th

THE morning was beautifully bright and clear. While dressing heard the breakfast bell, and received sundry intimations to descend and eat. However, I declined leaving my cabin until I had done dressing, during which time the ship weathered Point Judith, where the Atlantic comes in to the shore between the termination of Long Island and the southern extremity of Rhode Island. The water is generally rough here, and I had been prophesied an agreeable little fit of sea-sickness. But no such matter—we passed it very smoothly, and presently stopped at Newport, on Rhode Island, to leave and take up passengers.

The wind was keen and bracing; the blue waters, all curled and crisped under the arrow-like wind, broke into a thousand sapphire ridges tipped with silver foam, that drove away in sparkling showers before the bitter breath of the north.

We entered Providence river, and steamed along between Rhode Island and the main land, until we reached Providence, a town on the shore of Rhode Island, where we were to leave our boat and pursue our route by coach to Boston. I walked on deck with Captain Neill for an hour after breakfast, breasting the wind, which almost drove us back each time we turned up the deck towards the prow. After my walk I went in and righted my hair, which the wind had dressed "a la frantic", and sat in the sun with a book till we reached Providence.

When the crowd of passengers had ebbed away, we adjourned to our exclusive extra, which, to our great sorrow, could not take all our luggage after all. The distance from Providence to Boston is forty miles, but we were six and a half hours doing it over an excellent road. The weather was beautiful, but the country still sad and wintry looking. The spring is backwarder here than in New York by a full three weeks. The trees were all bare and leafless, except for the withered foilage of the black oaks, and the face of the country, with its monotonous rises, and brooks flowing through flat fields, reminded me of parts of Cumberland.

As we approached Boston, the country assumed a more cultivated aspect. The houses in the road-side villages were remarkably neat, and pretty and cottage-like, the land was well-farmed and the careful cultivation and stone walls, which perform the part of hedges here, together with the bleak look of the distances on each side, made me think of

Scotland. We entered Boston through a long road with houses on each side, making one fancy one's self in the town long before one reaches it. We did not arrive till half past six, so I went to my room and dressed for dinner. When I came to the drawing-room, I found the Hodgkinsons; dear Harriett was half crazy at seeing us again. Here we are in a new place!—how desolate and cheerless this constant changing of homes is. The scripture saith—"There is no rest for the wicked"—and truly, I never felt so convinced of my own wickedness as I have done since I have been in this country.

XVI

Monday, April 15th

WENT over to the theatre to rehearse *Fazio*, but Mr.
Barry, however, met us at the door, and assured me
that there was no necessity for my doing so till tomorrow.
At about half past four the horses came to the door. The
afternoon was lovely, and the roads remarkably good. I had
a fine, handsome, spirited horse, who pulled my hands to
pieces for want of being properly curbed. We rode out to
Cambridge, the University of Massachusetts, about three
miles distant from Boston. The village around it, with its
white cottages and meeting roads and the green lawns and
trees round the college, reminded me of England. We rode
to a place called Mount Auburn, a burial-ground, which
the Bostonians take pride in, and which is one of the lions
of the place. The whole place is at present in an unfinished
state, but its capabilities are very great. The enclosure is of
considerable extent—about one hundred acres—and contains several high hills and deep ravines. The whole is cut,
with much skill and good taste, by roads for carriages, and
small narrow footpaths. The various avenues are distinguished by the names of trees, as, Linden walk, Pine walk,
Beech walk. Already two or three white monuments are seen
glimmering palely through the woods, reminding one of the

solemn use to which this ground is consecrated, and which, for all its beauty, might seem a pleasure garden instead of a place of graves.

Mr. Hodgkinson delighted me very much, when he told me he was looking for a plot of earth in this cemetary which he intended to dedicate to poor English people, who might come out here, and die without the means of being decently laid to rest. We looked with this in view, at a patch of ground on the slope of a high hill, well shadowed with trees, and descending to a great depth to a dark pond, shining in the hollow like an emerald. 'Twas sad and touching to gaze on that earth, with the thought that amidst strangers, and in a strange land, the pity of a fellow-countryman should here allot to his brethren a grave in the quiet and solemn beauty of this hallowed ground. Our time was limited, so, after lingering for a short space along the narrow pathways that wind among the dwellings of the dead, we rode home.

My father and Dall were already gone to the theatre. I dressed and went over myself immediately. The play was begun and the house was not very full. The managers have committed the greatest piece of mismanagement imaginable—they advertise my father alone in *Hamlet* tonight, and instead of making me play alone tomorrow night, and so securing our attraction singly before we act together, we are *both* to act tomorrow in *Fazio*, which circumstance, of course, kept the house thin tonight. My father's Hamlet is very beautiful. 'Tis curious, that when I see him act I have none of the absolute feeling of contempt for the profession that I have when I am acting myself. What he does appears indeed like the work of an artist. I certainly respect acting more while I am seeing him act, than at any other time.

The Ophelia was perfectly beautiful; the eyes and brow of an angel, serene and calm, yet bright and piercing; a mouth chiselled like a Grecian piece of sculpture, with an expression of infinite refinement, and a figure that seemed to me to be perfectly porportioned. The audience are, on the whole, cold, very still and attentive, however, but when they do warm it is certainly very effective, for they shout and hurrah like mad.

Wednesday, April 17th

WROTE to Harriet, after dinner practised for an hour, and at half past five went off to the theatre. The house was crammed—the play, *The Stranger*. It is quite comical to see the people in the morning at the box office. Our window is opposite it, and 'tis a matter of the greatest amusement to me to watch them. They collect in crowds for upwards of an hour before the doors open, and when the bolt are drawn, there is a yelling and shouting as though the town were on fire. In they rush, thumping and pummelling one another, and not one comes out without rubbing his head, or his back, or showing a piteous rent in his clothes. I was surprised to see men of a very low order pressing forward to obtain boxes, but I find that they sell them again at an enormous increase to those who have not been able to obtain any. The better to carry on this traffic, these worthies smear their clothes with molasses and sugar, etc., in order to prevent any person of more decent appearance, or whose clothes are worth a cent, from coming near the box office. This is ingenious, and deserves a reward.

Our other window looks out upon a large church-yard, in the midst of which stands a cenotaph, erected by Franklin in honour of his father. Between the view of the playhouse, and the view of the burial ground, my contemplations are curiously tinged. This house—the Tremont—is admirably quiet and comfortable.

WALKED up to the State House. The day was anything but agreeable—a tremendous high wind—easterly of course, 'tis the only wind they have in Boston, and a burning sun tempered only be clouds of dust, in which, every two minutes, the whole world was shrouded. On entering the hall of the State House we confronted Chantry's statue of Washington, which stands in a recess immediately opposite the entrance. I saw it, how many years ago, in his studio in Pimlico! We proceeded to mount into the cupola, whence a very extensive view is obtained of the city and its surroundings—and a cruel height it was! I began it at full speed, like a wise woman, but before I got to the top was so out of breath, that I could hardly breathe at all. After all the day was hazy and not favourable for our purpose. The wind came through the windows of the lanthorn like a tornado; as my father observed, after the exertion of ascending, 'twas the very best place in the world for catching one's death of cold.

By the bye, on our way out to Mount Auburn we took the Charlestown road, and rode over Bunker Hill. They have begun a monument upon the spot where General Warren was killed, to commemorate the event. I felt strangely as I rode over that ground. Mr. Butler was the only American of our party, but though in the minority, he had rather the best of it. And this is where so much English blood was shed, thought I; for after all, 'twas all English blood—do as they can, they can never get rid of their stock. England and America ought not to be enemies—'tis unnatural while the same language is spoken in both lands. Until Americans have found a tongue for themselves, they must still be the children of old England, for they speak the words her children speak by the fireside of her homes. They may be proud of many things, these inheritors of a new world, but of nothing more than they are descended from Englishmen. Oh, England! noble, noble land!

At half past four we went to dine with the Hodgkinsons. Their house is very pretty and comfortable. When we first went in we were shown a couple of drawing rooms, in which there were beautiful marble copies of one or two of the famous statues. One of Canova's dancing girls, the glorious Diana, the crouching Venus, and the lovely antique Cupid and Psyche.

Tuesday, April 30th

WE rode down to the Chelsea Ferry, and crossed over the Charles river. The breath of the sea was delicious, as we crossed in one of the steam-boats constantly plying to and fro, and on the other side, as we rode towards the beach, it came greeting us delightfully from the wide waters. When we started from Boston the weather was intensely hot, and the day promised to be like the day before yesterday, a small specimen of the dog-days. We had about a five mile ride through some country that reminded me of Scotland. Now and then the dreary landscape was relieved by the golden branches of a willow tree, and the delicate pale peach blossoms, and tiny white buds in the apple orchards, peeping over some stone dyke, like a glance over the wall from the merry laughing spring.

So we reached Chelsea beach, a curving, flat, sandy shore, forming one side of a small bay which runs up between this land and a rocky peninsular, that stretches far out into the ocean, called Nahant. At the extremity of the basin lay glimmering a white, sunny town, by name Lynn. 'Tis quite absurd the starts and stares which the familiar names cause one for ever to make here. This small bay is beautifully smooth and peaceful, the shore is a shelving reach of hard, fine sand, nearly two miles long, and the wild waves are warded off in their violence from it by the rocky barrier of Nahant. Now happy I was to see the beautiful sea once more—to be once more galloping over the golden sands. How I do love the sea! For a short time my spirits seemed like uncaged birds; I rejoiced with all my might—I could have shouted aloud for delight. I galloped far along the sand, as close in to the water's restless edge as my horse could bear to go.

We rode two miles along the beach, and stopped at a little wooden hut, where, Mr. Hodgkinson told me, sports-men, who come to shoot plover along the flats by the shore, resort to dress their dinners and refresh themselves. Here we dismounted and lay in the sun with the fresh, sweet blessed breath of heaven fanning us. My horse thought proper to break his bridle and walk himself off through the fields. They followed him with corn and various induce-ments. Pierce Butler and I, mean time, ran down to the water, collecting interesting relics, muscle [sic] shells, quartz, pebbles, and sea-weed. Finally we remounted and returned home.

As we rode down a pleasant lane towards the Salem road, we met a large crowd of country-people busily employed in raising the framework of a house. In this part of the coun-try, the poorer class of people build their houses. In this part of the country, the poorer class of people build their houses, or rather, the wooden frames of their houses, en-tirely before they set them up. When the skeleton is fin-ished they call together all their neighbours to assist in the raising, which is an event of much importance, and gen-erally ends in merry-making. The filling up the outline of the house, which they do with boards here, is an after work—the frame seems to be the material part of the building, and slight enough too, I thought, for protection against these bitter east winds.

We reached home at about half past two. The play was— *Much Ado About Nothing.* The house was spoilt by the fair which the ladies have been getting up for the blind, and which was lighted and open for inspection previous to to-morrow, when the sale is to take place.

Wednesday, May 1st

MR. Hodgkinson came in the morning, and I settled to call at eleven for Mrs. Hodgkinson to go to the fair. We drove to Faneuil Hall, a building opposite the market, which was appropriated to the uses of the fair. The crowd was so dense round the steps, that we found it impossible to approach them, and wisely gave up the attempt, determining to take our drive and then come back and try our fortune later. We drove down to the Chelsea beach. The day was bleak and cold, though bright, with a cutting east wind. After taking a good race along the bright, creaming edge, we returned to the carriage, and drove again to the fair, which we managed at last to enter. The whole thing was crowd, crush and confusion, to my bewildered eyes. We got upon a platform behind the stalls, and squeezed our way to Mrs. Hodgkinson's shop, where my father had desired me to buy him a card-case, which I did. I found Harriet installed in her stall, where I bought one or two things, and having emptied my purse, came away. After dinner, Mr. Butler came in, and showed us some things he had bought at the fair. I thought the prices enormous, but the money is well spent in itself, or rather, on its ultimate object.

I HAVE taken several enormous rides round Boston, and am more and more delighted with its environs, which are now in full flush of blossoming, as sweet, and fresh, and lovely as anything can be. On Saturday rode to the Blue Hills, a distance of upwards of twelve miles. The roads round this place are almost as good as roads in England, and the country altogether reminds me of that dear little land. These Blue Hills were, a few years ago, a wilderness of forest—the favourite resort of rattlesnakes. But the trees have been partly cleared, and though 'tis still a wild, desolate region, clothed with firs, and uncheered by a human habitation, its more savage tenants have disappeared with the thick coverts in which they nestled, and we rode to the summit of the hill without seeing anything in the shape of Eve's enemy.

The view from the mountain is magnificent, yet I do not believe the elevation to be very extraordinary, although as I looked down it seemed to me as though the world was stretched at my feet. The various villages, with their blossoming orchards, looked like patches of a snow scene. The river wound, like a silver snake, all round the fields. The little lakes lay diminished to drops of blue light, and the lesser mountains rose below us like the waves of a dark sea.

The mountain itself is formed of granite, of which large slabs appeared through the turf and brushwood. I looked in vain for what I found in such abundance on the Portland hill—the sweet wild thyme. I thought I would find some of it among the stony rifts, where it loves to cling, but I was disappointed. Indeed I met with a much more severe disappointment than that. The turf was thickly strewn with clumps of violets, the very same in form and colour, as our own sweet wood violet. I stopped in an ecstasy to gather them, but found they were utterly scentless—mere pretences of violets. A violet without fragrance! a wild one too!—the thing's totally unnatural! I flung the little purple thing away in a rage. I have since found cowslips with the same entire absence of fragrance. The heat and cold of this climate chill or wither everything, and almost all the flowers which are common and sweet, growing in the moist soil of England, seem reared with difficulty here, and lose their great fragrance, their soul, as it were, under the extreme influence of this sky.

There are, I believe, no primroses, no wild thyme and no heather, that grow naturally in this country. I do not remember to have seen either wild honeysuckle, or clematis, both of which are so abundant with us. The laurestinus, rosemary, and monthly roses, all of which are so common in England, growing out-of-doors all the years round, are kept in hot-houses during the winter, even as far south as Philadelphia. The common garden flowers— roses, pinks, are far less abundant and less fragrant than with us.

There were many wild things growing on this mountain, that for beauty, and delicacy of form and colour, would have found an honourable place in our conservatories, but they had not the slightest perfume, and I took no delight in them. A scentless flower is a monster. Oh the lilies of the valley, the primroses, the violets, the fresh, fragrant blush rose, the purple lilac bloom, the golden cowslips, of a morning at the close of May in England! the fulness of the sweetness that loads the temperate air, as it breathes over the fresh lawns of that flower garden!

XVII

Visit to a quarry near Boston—Dr. Channing's opinion of
Shakespeare—A meeting with Black Hawk—A visit to Governor
Kemble's house and the iron works—Fanny gets a soaking in
a waterfall

Thursday, May 2nd (cont.)

I TOOK another long ride to a quarry ten miles from
Boston, whence the granite, which is much used in
Boston for building, is drawn. I started at six in the morning, and rode about twenty miles before breakfast, which I
think was a piece of virtue bordering on heroism. To be
sure I had my reward, for anything so sweet as the whole
world, at about half past six, I never beheld. The dew was
yet fresh upon tree and flower—the roads were shady and
cool—the dust had not yet been disturbed. A mild, soft,
full breeze blew over the flowery earth, and rosy apple blossoms stirred on the rocking boughs against the serene and
smiling sky. They have in this country neither nightin-
gales, thrushes, linnets nor blackbirds—at least none with
the same notes as ours.

The quarry we visited is an extensive vein of fine, dark-
coloured granite. We dismounted and walked among the
workmen to see them at their various processes. This quarry,
and one at a short distance, merely supply the blocks of
granite, which, being detached from the main stone, are
piled upon cars, and sent down an inclined plane to the
rail-road, by means of a powerful chain, which acts at once
as a support and check, suffering the load to proceed slowly

down the declivity, and at the same time sending up from the bottom, upon another track, the empty car, from which the granite has been unloaded below, as the buckets of a well are drawn up and down.

The rough blocks of granite are conveyed by horses, in these same rail-road cars, to smaller quarries below, where they are wrought and shaped for their appointed uses. After looking down from the summit of the granite rock upon the country which lay smiling for many a sunny mile of flowery earth and sparkling sea below, and wandering about the works, which are interesting and curious, we remounted and rode home. The country we rode through was extremely pretty—so indeed I think all the country around Boston is; the only deficiency is water—running water, I mean, for there are several beautiful pools in its vicinity—and turn which way you will, the silver shield of the sea shining against the horizon, is a lovely feature of the landscape. But there are no rivulets, no brooks, no sparkling, singing water—courses to refresh one's senses, as one rides across the fields and through the woodlands.

Mr. Webster called on us Sunday last. He is very enchanting. I wish it had been my good fortune to see him oftener—one of the great men of this country, he would have been a first-rate man all the world over. Like all first-rate people, there is a simplicity and a total want of pretension about him tht is very delightful. He gave us description of Niagara, which conveyed to us an exact idea of the natural position and circumstances which render these falls so wonderful. Most describers launch forth into vague and intangible rhapsodies, which, after all, convey no idea but water in the abstract. But he gave me, by his few simple words, a more real impression of the stupendous cataract, than all that was ever written or spoken of waterfalls before, not excepting Bryon's Terni.

Last Saturday I dined at the Webster's, where, for my greater happiness, I sat between John Irving Adams and Mrs. Webster. Mr. Adams, speaking of Knowles' *Hunchback*, said—"Well, after all, its no matter. The author evidently understands stage effect and dramatic situations, and so on, but as for writing, it's by no means as good as Shakespeare". I looked at the man in amazement, and suggested to him that Shakespeare did not grow on every bush. Mr. Adams presently assured me that he was no worshipper of Shakespeare, but then said that *Othello* was disgusting, *King Lear* ludicrous, and *Romeo and Juliet* childish nonsense. I swallowed half a pint of water, and nearly my tumbler too, and remained silent—for what could I say?

The climate of this place is dreadful. The night before last the weather was so warm that, with my window open, I was obliged to take half the clothes off the bed. Last night was so cold, that with the window shut, and with additional covering, I could scarce get to sleep for the cold. This is terrible, and forms a serious drawback upon the various attractions of Boston, and to me it has many. The houses are like English houses, the common is like Constitution Hill, Beacon Hill is like a bit of Park Lane, and Summer Street, now that the chestnut trees are in bloom, is perfectly beautiful. It is in itself a lovely place, and the country round it is charming. The people are intellectual, and have been most abundantly good-natured and kind to me.

New York, May 1833

I HAVE seen Dr. Channing, who, in his outward man, bears but little token of his inward greatness. Miss Sedgwick had prepared me for an exterior over which debility and sickness had triumphed for some years. But, thought I, there must be eyes and a brow, and there the spirit will surely be seen upon its throne. But the eyes were small grey ones, with an expression which struck me at first as more akin to shrewdness of judgement, than genius, and the loftier qualities of the mind. And though the brow and the forehead were those of an intellectual person they had neither the expanse nor conformation I had imagined.

The subject of our conversation, though sufficiently natural for him to choose addressing one of my craft, did not appear to me to be a happy one for his own powers—perhaps I though so because I differed from him. He talked about the stage and acting in as unreal and mistaken a manner as possible. Had he expressed himself unknowingly about acting, that would not have surprised me, for he can have no means of judging it, not having frequented the theatre for some years past. Lawrence was the only man I ever heard speak about the stage with understanding and accuracy. I have heard the very cleverest men in England talk the greatest stuff imaginable about actors and acting.

But to return to Dr. Channing. He said he had not thought much upon the subject, but what it appeared to him feasible and highly desirable, to take detached passages and scenes from the finest dramatic writers, and have them well declaimed in comparatively private assemblies—this as a wholesome substitute for the stage, of which he said he did not approve. He thought this the best method of obtaining the intellectual pleasure and profit to be derived from fine dramatic works, without the illusion and excitement belonging to theatrical exhibitions.

My horror was so unutterable at this proposition, that I believe my replies to it were all but incoherent. What! take one of Shakespeare's plays bit by bit, break it piece-meal, in order to make recitals of it!—destroy the marvellous unity of one of his magnificent works, to make patches of declamation! If the stage is evil, put it away, and put away with it those writings which properly belong to it and to nothing else. But do not take dramatic compositions, things full of present action and emotion, to turn them into recitations and mutilated ones, too. Get other poems to declaim, no matter how vivid or impassioned in their descriptions, so their form be not dramatic. It is not to be supposed that the effect proper and natural to a fine dramatic conception can be preserved, when the language is merely declaimed without the assistance of distance, dress, scenic effects— all the appertainings that the author has reckoned upon to work out his idea.

Dr. Channing mentioned the dagger soliloquy in *Macbeth*, as an instance which would admit of being executed after his idea, saying that that, well read by any person in a drawing-room, would have all the effect necessary or desirable. I remember hearing my aunt Siddons read the scenes of the witches in Macbeth, and while doing so was obliged to cover my eyes, so that her velvet gown, modern cap and spectacles, might not disturb the wild and sublime images that her magnificent voice and recitation were conjuring up around me. If a man professes to tell you a story, no matter what, say the story of Romeo and Juliet, and sits in a modern drawing-room, in modern costume, it matters not—*he* is no part of his story—you do not connect him with his narrative—his appearance in no way clashes with your train of thought—you are not thinking of him, but of the people he is talking about. But if a man in a modern drawing-room, but in modern costume, were to get up and begin reciting the balcony scene in *Romeo and Juliet*, I think the case would be altered. However, never having heard such a proposal before, I had not thought much about it, and only felt a little stunned at the idea of Shakespeare's histories being broken into fragments.

AT a little after ten, Mr. Butler came to take us to see the savages. We drove down, Dall, my father, he and I, to their hotel. We found, even at that early hour, the portico, passage and staircase, thronged with gazers upon the same errand as ourselves. We made our way, at length, into the presence chamber—a narrow little dark room, with all the windows shut, crowded with people, come to stare at their fellow wild beasts. Upon a sofa, sat Black Hawk, a diminutive, shrivelled-looking old man, with an appearance of much activity in his shrunk limbs, and a calmness and dignified self-composure in his manner, which, in spite of his want of size and comeliness, was very striking. Next to him sat a young man, the adopted son of his brother the Prophet, whose height and breadth, and peculiar gravity of face and deportment were those of a man of nearly forty, whereas he is little more than half that age. The undisturbed seriousness of his countenance was explained to me by their keeper thus—he had, it seems, the day before, indulged rather too freely in the delights of champagne, and was suffering just retribution in the shape of a head-ache.

Next to him sat Black Hawk's son, a noble, big young creature, like a fine Newfoundland puppy, with a handsome scornful face, which yet exhibited more familiarity and good-humoured amusement at what was going on, than any of the rest. His hair was powdered on the top, and round the ears with bright vermillion-coloured powder, and knots of scarlet berries or beads, hung like ear-rings on each side of his face. A string of glass beads was tied round his naked throat, and he was wrapped in a large blanket, which completely concealed his form. He seemed much alive to what was going on, conversed freely in his own language with his neighbour, and laughed aloud once or twice, which rather surprised me, as I had heard so much of their immovable gravity. The costume of the other young man was much the same, except that his hair was not adorned.

Black Hawk himself, had on a blue cloth surtout, scarlet leggings, a black silk neck handkerchief, and ear-rings. His appearance was altogether not unlike that of an old French gentleman. Beside him, on a chair, sat one of his warriors, wrapped in a blanket, with a cotton handkerchief whisped around his head. At one of the windows apart from their companions, with less courtesy in their demeanour, and a great deal of sullen savageness in their aspects, sat the great warrior and the prophet of the tribe—the latter is Black Hawk's brother. I cannot express the feeling of commiseration and disgust which the whole scene gave me. That men such as ourselves, creatures with like feelings, like perceptions, should be brought as strange animals at a show, to be gazed at the livelong day by succeeding shoals of gaping folk, struck me as totally unfitting. The cold dignity of the old chief, and the malignant scowl of the prophet, expressed the indecency and irksomeness of such a situation. Then, to look at those two young savages, with their fine muscular proportions, and think of them cooped up the whole day long, in this hot prison-house full of people, made my heart ache. How they must loathe the sight of these narrow walls, and the sound of these strange voices, how they must sicken for their unmeasured range of wilderness!

The gentleman who seemed to have charge of them, pressed me to go up and shake hands with them, as everybody else in the room did, but I refused to do so, from literal compassion, and unwillingness to add to the wearisome toil they were made to undergo. As we were departing, however, they reiterated their entreaties that we would go up and shake hands with them—so I did. Black Hawk and the young men received our courtesy with great complaisance, but when we went to the great warrior and the prophet, they seemed exceedingly loath to receive our hands. I instinctively withdrew my hand, but when my father offered his, the savage's face relaxed into a smile, and he met his greeting readily. I wonder what pleased him about my father's greeting, whether it was his large size or not. I had a silver vinaigrette in my pouch, which I gave Black Hawk's son, by way of a keepsake—it will make a charming present for his squaw.

Sunday, June 30th

ROSE at four, but after looking at my watch, resumed my slumbers till six, when I started up, much dismayed to find it so late, and having dressed as fast as I could, we set off for the steam-boat. The morning was the brightest possible, the glorious waters that meet before New York were all like rivers of light blazing with the reflected radiance of the morning sky. We had no sooner set foot on board the steam-boat, than a crowd of well-known faces surrounded us. I was introduced to Mr. Trelawney, and Mr. William Kemble, brother of our host at Cold Spring. Mr. Trelawney came and stood by me for a considerable time after we started. It is agreeable to talk to him, because he has known and seen so much. He has traversed the world in every direction, and been the friend of Byron and Shelley. The common mind that had enjoyed the same opportunities, must have acquired something from intercourse with such men, but he is an uncommon man, and it is very interesting to hear him talk of what he has seen, and those he has known.

When we reached West Point, Mr. Governor Kemble was waiting with his boat to convey us over to Cold Spring, and accordingly bidding our various acquaintances and companions farewell, we rowed over out of the course of the river, into the sunny bay it forms among the hills, to our kinsman's abode. Mr. Kemble's place is a lovely little nook, situated on the summit of a rise, on the brink of the placid curve of water formed here by the river, and which extends from the main current about a mile into the mountains, .ending in a wide marsh. The house, though upon a hill, is looked down upon, and locked in by the highlands around it, so that it seems to be at the bottom of a valley. From the verandah of his house, through various frames which he has cut among the plantations around the lawn, exquisite glimpses appeared of the mountains, the little bay, the glorious Hudson itself, with the graceful boats, their white sails coming through the rocky passes, where the river could not be detected, as though they were sailing through the valleys of the earth.

The day was warm, but a fresh breeze stirred the boughs, and cooled the air. My father and Dall seemed overcome with drowsiness, and lay on the verandah with half-closed eyes, peeping at the dream-like scene around them. I was not inclined to rest, and Mr. Kemble having promised to show me some falls at a short distance from the house, he and his brother, and I, set forth thither. We passed through the iron-works, and as 'twas Sunday, everything except a bright water-course, laughing and singing as it ran, was still. They took me over the works, showed me the iron frames of large mill wheels, the machinery and process of boring the cannon, the model of an iron forcing pump, the casting houses, and all the wonders of their manufactory. All mechanical science is very interesting to me, when I have the opportunity of seeing the detail of it, and comprehending, by illustrations presented to my eyes, the technical terms used by those conversing with me.

We left those dark abodes, and their smouldering fires, and strange and powerful-looking instruments, and taking a path at the foot of the mountains, skirted the marsh for some time, and then struck into the woods. We ascended tremendous stony path, at the top of which we threw ourselves down to pant, and looked below through a narrow rent in the curtain of leaves around us, on the river, the rocks, and mountains, bright with the noon-day splendour of the unclouded sky. After resting here for a few moments, we arose and climbed again, through the woods, to the brow of the hill, where stands the Highland School. Passing through the ground surrounding it, we joined a road skirting a deep ravine, from the bottom of which the waters called to me. I was wild to go down, but my companions would not let me.

We followed the path, which began to decline, and presently a silver thread of gushing water, ran like a frightened child across our way, and flung itself down into the glen. At last we reached the brown, golden-looking stream. Mr. Kemble was exhorting us to take an upper path, which he said would bring us to the foot of the fall. But I was not to be seduced away from the side of the rivulet, and insisted upon crossing it then and there, through the water, over moss-capped stones, across fallen trees, which had chocked up the brook with their leafy bridges. So, striving on, we reached the end and aim of our journey, the waterfall.

We stood on the brink of a pool, about forty feet across, and varying in depth from about three to seven or eight feet; it was perfectly circular, and closed around with a wall of rock about thirty feet high, in whose crevices trees hung fearlessly, clothing the grey stone with a soft curtain of vivid green. Immediately opposite the brook, the water came tumbling over this rocky wall in three distinct streams, which striking the projecting ledges of iron-looking stone, at different angles, met within eight or ten feet of the pool, and fell in a mingled sheet of foam. The water broke over the rocks like a shower of splintered light, the spray sprang up in the sunlight, and fell again all glittering into the dark basin below, that gleamed like a magic jewel set in the mossy earth.

As I gazed up in perfect ecstacy, an uncontrollable desire seized me to clamber up the rocks by the side of the fall, and so reach the top of it. My companions laughed incredulously as I expressed my determination to do so, but followed where I led, until they became well assured that I was in earnest. Remonstrance and representation of impossibility having been tried in vain, Mr. William Kemble prepared to guide me, and Mr. Governor Kemble, with my bag, parasol, and bonnet in charge, returned to the edge of the pool to watch our progress. Away we went over the ledges of the rocks, with nothing but damp leaves and slippery roots of trees for footing. At one moment the slight covering of mould on which I had placed my foot, crumbled from beneath it, and I swung over the water by a young sapling, which upheld me well, and by which I recovered footing and balance. We had now reached the immediate side of the waterfall, and my guide began ascending the slippery, slanting rocks down which it fell. I followed; in an instance I was soaked through with the spray—my feet slipped—I had no hold—he was up above me—the pool far below. With my head bowed against the foam and water, I was feeling where next to tread, when a bit of rock, that my companion had thought firm, broke beneath his foot, and came falling down beside me into the stream. I paused, for I was frightened. I looked up for a moment, but was blinded by the water, and could not see where my guide was. I looked down the slanting ledge we had climbed, over which the white water was churning angrily. "Shall I come down again?", I cried to Mr. Kemble, who was anxiously looking up at our perilous path. "Give me your hand!", shouted his brother above me. I lifted my head and turned towards him, and a dazzling curtain of spray and foam fell over my face. "I cannot see you", I replied, "I cannot go on—I do not know what to do!" "Give me your hand!", he exclaimed again, and I planting one foot on a ledge of rock so high as to lift me off the other, held up my arm to him. But my limbs were so strained from his height above me, that I had no power to spring or move, either up or down. I felt my presence of mind going, I knew that to go down was impossible, except headlong—the ascent therefore must be persevered in.

"Are you steady, quite, quite steady!", I inquired; he replied, "Yes", and holding out his hand, I locked mine in it, and bade him draw me up. But he had not calculated upon my weight—my slight appearance had deceived him—and as I bore upon his arm, we both of us slipped—I turned as sick as death, and only cried out, "Recover yourself! recover yourself!, I am safe!", which I was, upon a rocky rim about three inches wide, with my arm resting on the falling stump of a blasted tree. He did recover his balance, and again holding out his hand, drew me up beside where he was sitting on the edge of the rocks in the water. In the midst of the rushing brook, I wrung out my handkerchief triumphantly at Mr. Kemble, which was rather a comical consideration, as I was literally dripping from head to foot. As soon as he saw us safe, he scrambled up through the woods to the road, and we doing the same, we all met on the dusty highway, where we congratulated each other on our perseverance and success, and laughed exceedingly at my soaked situation. We determined not to pass through the Highland School grounds, but kept to the main road for the advantage of sun and wind, the combined influences of which presently dried my frock and handkerchief. When I reached home, I ran up stairs, and dressed for dinner, and after dinner, I came up to my room, and slept very profoundly until summoned to coffee, which we drank on the verandah. At about eight o'clock, the sun had left the sky, but his warm mantle lay over the western clouds, and hung upon the rocks and woody mountain sides. A gently breeze was stirring the trees round where we sat, and through the thick branches of a chestnut tree, the silver disc of the full moon looked placidly down upon us.

We set out strolling through the woods, and took our way through the twilight paths. When we reached the Roman Catholic chapel our host is building by the river, the silent thoughtful, mountains were wrapped in deep shadows, and the broad waters shone like a sheet of silver in the moonlight. We sat down on a cannon lying on the shore, and Mr. Kemble ran off to order a boat. We got in, Abel rowing, and they put me at the helm. But owing to Mr. Kemble's misdirections—who seemed extremely amused by my awkwardness, and took delight in bothering poor Abel by making me steer all awry—we made but little progress, and that rather crab-wise, backing, and sidelong, and turning, as thought the poor boat had been a politician. Full of my own contemplations I kept steering round and round, and so we wandered as purposeless as the night air over the smooth waters, till near eleven o'clock, when we made for shore and slowly turned home.

XVIII

*Testing the cannon—To Troy by steamboat—In Albany—Along the
canal to Utica—To Trenton by carriage—Walk to the Trenton
Falls—Back to Utica and on for 76 miles to Auburn—The Kembles'
carriage overturns on the way to Niagara—Niagara at last!*

Monday, July 1st, 1833

MR. Governor Kemble came over from West Point, as
they were going to prove some cannon, that had not
yet been fired, and some time passed in the various prepa-
rations for so doing. At length we were summoned down to
the water side, to see the success of the experiment. The
cannon lay obliquely along the curve line of the little bay,
their muzzles pointed to the high gravelly bank, into which
they fired. The guns were loaded with very heavy charges,
and as soon as we were safely placed so as to see and hear,
they were fired. The sound was glorious; the first heavy peal,
and then echo after echo.

They ended in discharging all the cannon at once, which
made a most glorious row, and kept the mountains grum-
bling with its echoes for some minutes after the discharge.
All the pieces were sound, which was highly satisfactory,
as upon each one that flaws in firing, Mr. Kemble loses the
cost of the piece.

Mr. Kemble proposed an admirable plan, that of walking down to the water's side, and taking a boat upon the
Hudson, and so avoiding the long walk home. We called
at the Highland School, where the worthy man who keeps
it, received us with infinite civility, put us into a delicious

cool room, and gave us some white hermitage and water to drink, which did us all manner of good. We then descended to the river, and after some difficulty and delay, got a boat and rowed home.

Tuesday, July 2nd 1833

PACKED up my bag, took a cup of tea, went and gathered some flowers, bade a very unwilling farewell to the pretty place, and rowed over to West Point, where Mr. Trelawney was waiting for us. We breakfasted at ten, and went down to meet the boat. I took out my work, and Mr. Trelawney sat down by us. He has seen such things, and known such people, that it is greatly worthwhile to listen to him. Everything he says of Shelley and Byron confirms my impression of them.

The scenery of the Hudson immediately beyond West Point loses much of its sublimity, though no beauty. The river widens and the rugged summits of the Highlands melt gradually into a softer and more undulating outline. On the left, presently we began to see the blue outline of the Catskill mountains, towering into the hot sky, and looking most blessedly cool and dark amid the fervid glowing of the noonday world.

At about half past three, the sky became suddenly and thickly overcast, the awning which sheltered the upper deck was withdrawn, and every preparation made for a storm. The pale angry-looking clouds lay heaped like chalk upon a leaden sky, and presently one red lightning dipped down into the woods like a fiery snake falling from the heavens. At the same time, a furious gust of wind and torrent of rain rushed down the mountain side. We scuttled down to the lower deck as fast as we could, but the storm met us at the bottom of the stairs, and in an instant I was drenched.

Chairs, tables, everything was overturned by the gust, and the boat was running with water in every direction. I stood by the door of the furnace, and dried leisurely, talking the while to Mr. Trelawney, who is sun burnt enough to warm one through with a look.

We reached Albany at about half past five in the afternoon, and went to a house the Hosacks had recommended to us. At about seven they gave us dinner, and immediately after I came up to my room. I was so exhausted with fatigue and a violent cold and cough, that I literally fell on the floor and slept till dark.

Saturday, July 6th

WHEN we were in the steamboat, going up to Troy, Trelawney put a letter into my hands, which he told me was written by the mother of Allegra, Bryon's child. The letter was remarkable only for more straightforwardness and conciseness than is usual in women's letters. I do not know whether Trelawney gave it to me to read on that account alone, or because it contained allusions to wild and interesting adventures of his own—perhaps there was a mingling of motives.

We reached Troy in about twenty minutes, and walked up into the town to procure some species of vehicle for our progress to the Falls. There was none ready, and while one was being procured, a man who was standing near us very civilly invited us to come into his shop and sit down, which we did readily. The shop we were in was a china store, and the nice cold crockery made one cool to look at it—the weather was roasting. The storekeeper assured us the Trojans were an exceedingly refined and literary set of folks, and that the society, in point of these two advantages, was no whit behind Boston—there's for Boston!

We obtained a coach, and crossed a ferry such I had never seen before, worked by horses. Poor wretches! After crossing the ferry, we drove about five miles through some gentle smiling lands that made one feel very charitable. After wandering about for some time, we sat ourselves down on a high, grassy knoll just above the Falls. We returned in time, we flattered ourselves, to meet the steamboat which leaves Troy for Albany at four. But just as we were crossing the ferry, the steamer ran past us, leaving us with eyes and mouths wide open, very much bothered as to how we were to get down to Albany. Dall proposed a row boat, and the sense of the company seemed to agree thereto. But upon driving to the inn where we hired our carriage, we were assured that there was no such thing to be had. Whereupon my father, good easy man, got into the coach again.

Mr. Trelawney, however, had absconded, and remained gone so long, that I began to think he had perhaps started to swim down the river, when he appeared, informing us he had gotten a boat for us. We jumped readily out of the coach, and though my father had actually made a bargain for the hire of it, to convey us to Albany, with the inn-keeper, and moreover given him the money, the righteous man refunded the dollars! Our row back was delightful, the evening was calm and lovely beyond description.

We reached Albany in very good time for dinner. Mr. Trelawney dined with us—what a savage he is in some respects. He's a curious being, a description of him would puzzle anyone who had never seen him. A man with proportions of a giant for strength and agility, taller, straighter and broader than most men, yet with the most listless indolent carelessness of gait, and an uncertain wandering way of dropping his feet to the ground, as if he didn't know where he was going, and didn't much wish to go anywhere. His face is as dark as a Moor's, with a wild strange look about the eyes and forehead, and a mark like a scar upon his cheek. His whole appearance gives one an idea of toil, hardship, peril and wild adventure. The expression of his mouth is remarkably mild and sweet, and his voice is extremely low and gentle. His hands are as brown as a labourer's; he never profanes them with gloves, but wears two strange musical looking rings—one of them, which he showed me, is made of elephant's hair.

Monday, July 8th

AFTER breakfast, went to rehearsal. Mr. Trelawney came with us. The actors were one and all reading their parts, the lady who played Charlotte was the only exception, she was perfect. As I sat on the stage, between my scenes, a fat, good-tempered looking man accosted me. Having ascertained that I was myself, proceeded to accuse me of having, as Mrs. Haller, pronounced the word "industry" with the accent on the middle syllable, as, "indus-try", adding that he had already quoted my authority to several people for the emphasis and begging to know my "exquisite" reason therefore. It was in vain that I urged that it must have been a mistake if I said so. I never meant to say so, that I was very sorry for having said so, that I would never say so again. Between each of my humblest apologies my accuser merely replied, "but you *did* say 'industry'", with an inflexible pertinacity of condemnation, which was not a whit softened by my sincere confessions. Mr. Trelawney told me the man was a newspaper editor, but I think he looked too fat and good-tempered for that.

The play was *The Gamester*, the house was very full. At the end of the play they called for my father, and civilly desired we would act *The Hunchback*. As however, we had not the dresses for it, he declined but promised we would return hereafter.

Tuesday, July 9th

AFTER breakfast, the day being extremely fine, Mr. Trelawney urged us to go out and take a walk. So forth we set, my father and I leading the way, and Dall and Mr. Trelawney following. We crossed the river, and arrived at the top of a delightful breezy knoll, opposite a tiny waterfall, the rocks and basin of which were picturesque, but the water had been turned off to turn a mill. The hill where we stood, commanded a beautiful view of the Hudson, Albany, and the shores stretching away into the sunny distance. We strolled through the woods and along the high road, with the sweet smell of mellow hay keeping us company the while. Mr. Trelawney killed us with laughing, with an account he gave us of some of Bryon's sayings and doings, which were just as whimsical and eccentrick, as unamiable, but very funny. Tomorrow we start for Utica, and Mr. Trelawney comes with us, I am glad of it, I like him.

Wednesday, July 19th

JUST as we were getting into the rail-road coach for Schenectady, a parcel was put into my hand. It was a letter from Catherine Sedgwick, and Pellico's *Mie Prigioni*—I was glad of it. At Schenectady we dined. By the bye, I must not forget to mention the civility we met from the people who kept the house. There have been so many instances given, of the discomfort and discourteousness which travellers encounter in America, that 'tis but justice to record the reverse when one meets with it. For my own part, with very few exceptions, I have hitherto met with nothing but civility and attention of every description.

We proceeded by canal to Utica, which distance we performed in a day and a night, starting at two from Schenectady, and reaching Utica the next day at noon. I like travelling by the canal boats very much. Our's was not crowded, and the country through which we passed being delightful, the placid, moderate gliding through it, at about four miles an hour, seemed to me infinitely preferable to the noise of wheels, the rumble of a coach, and the jerking of bad roads.

Mr. Trelawney read Don Quixote to us. He reads very peculiarly, slowly and with marked emphasis. He has a strong feeling of humour, as well of poetry—in fact they belong to each other.

The valley of the Mohawk, through which we crept the whole sunshining day, is beautiful from beginning to end, fertile, soft, rich, and occasionally approaching sublimity and grandeur, in its rocks and hanging woods. We had a lovely day, and a soft blessed sunset, which threw one of the most exquisite effects of light and colour I ever remember to have seen, over the water, and through the sky. The sun had scarce been down ten minutes from the horizon, when the deck was wet with the heaviest dew possible, which drove us down to the cabin.

Here I fell fast asleep, till awakened by the cabin girl's putting her arms affectionately round me, and telling me that I might come and have first choice of a berth for the night, in the horrible hencoop alloted to the female passengers. I was too sleepy to avail myself of this courtesy, but as I stood cowering in a corner, half asleep, half crying, the cabin girl came to me again, and entreated me to let her make a bed for me. However, upon my refusing to undress before so much company, or lie down in such narrow neighbourhood, she put Dall and myself in a small closet, where there were four empty berths, where I presently fell asleep. Dall, wrapped up in a shawl, sat till morning under the half open hatchway, breathing damp starlight.

Thursday, July 11th

DALL'S exclamations woke me in the morning. The day was breaking when we approached Little Falls, a place where the placid, gentle character of the Mohawk becomes wild and romantic. When we arrived at Utica, I gave the nice cabin girl my silver needle case. She took my gift, and throwing her arms round my neck, kissed me very fervently for it. She was a very singular and striking-looking person. As for Mr. Trelawney, he fell in love with her forthwith, and I think had half a mind to settle on the Mohawk and make her his fellow-farmer. At Utica we dined, and after dinner I slept profoundly.

Friday, July 12th

WE all breakfasted together, and immediately after got into an open carriage, and set off for Trenton. The day was bright and sunny, the country all around us was smiling in rich beauty. About seven miles from Utica, we stopped to water the horses at a lonely roadside house. We alighted, and without ceremony strolled into the garden, a mere wilderness of overgrown sweetbriar, dog-roses, and flaunting red poppies, overshadowed by some orchard trees— from which we stole sundry half-ripe cherries.

We got into the carriage again, and the remaining eight miles of our journey were as beautiful as the preceding ones had been. At last we reached the house at which vistors to the Falls are put up, a large, comfortable dwelling, kept by a couple of nice young people. We ordered dinner, and set forth to the Falls, with our host for guide. We crossed a small wood immediately adjoining the house, and descending several flights of steps, we presently stood on the brink of the channel, where the water was boiling along. We walked on steadily, and presently we arrived at the first fall.

After standing before the tumbling mass of water for a length of time, we climbed to the shore above and went on. Mr. Trelawney flung himself down under a roof of rock by the waterfall. My father, Dall, and the guide went on, out of sight, and Mr. Butler and I loitered by the rapid waters. When we came to the beautiful circular fall, we crept down to a narrow ridge, and sat with our feet hanging over the black cauldron. I began to grow dizzy with the sound and motion of the churning darkness beneath us, and begged to move. I was in an agony lest we should slip from the narrow, dripping ledges along which we crawled. We wandered on, and stopped again upon a rocky shelf overhanging the torrent, beside the blasted and prostrate trunk of a large tree. I was tired with walking, and Mr. Butler lifted me up to seat me on the fallen tree.

At length we rejoined the whole party, sitting by a narrow channel where the water looked like ink. Beyond this our guide said it was impossible to go. I was thirsty, and the guide having given me a beautiful strawberry and a pale bluebell that he had found, like a couple of jewels, I devoured the one, and then going down to the water's edge, we dipped the fairy cup in, and drank the cold clear water.

When we were all rested, we rose to retrace our steps. Our guide was a man of some cultivation and of much natural refinement. He pointed out to me the spot beside the torrent where he said he had read all Byron's works—this pleased me. We returned to the house and dined. After dinner I strolled into the garden—it was in disorder and looked like a wilderness. Then about sun-set I wandered into the wood to the top of the steps leading to the waterfall, where far below, I could hear its sweet voice singing as it passed away. I remained standing there till the carriage was announced. Just before we went away, our host gave me a small piece of crystal, which is found among the rocks here, which I believe present many curious geological phenomena.

It grew dark long before we reached Utica. Half the way I sang, the other half I slept, in spite of the ruts five fathoms deep, and all the joltings of these evil ways.

Saturday, July 13th

WE left Utica at six o'clock, in our Exclusive Extra. We were to go as far as Auburn, a distance of seventy-six miles. The day was very beautiful, but very hot. At Vernon we had a very good breakfast. While the coach was getting ready, Pierce Butler and I began wandering about, but the place did not look promising, and the heat was intense. In about an hour we set off again. The country was very rich and beautiful, and at every knoll backed by woodlands and skirted by golden grain fields, Mr. Trelawney exclaimed, "Come, we will have a farm here!".

My father and Mr. Trelawney had long argumentations about acting; the latter is a vehement admirer of Kean's, and of course, that being the case, matter of debate was not wanting. It was all extremely pleasant and profitable, and while the sun shone, and we all kept our tempers, nothing could do better. Pierce Butler amused me by telling me portions of Trelawney's book, *The Adventures of a Younger Son,* with which he had been extremely charmed, and which I remember beginning on board ship, as we crossed from England.

At about half past three, we arrived at a place called Syracuse, where, stopping to change horses, my father observed that there were two different routes to our point of destination, and desired our driver to take that which passes through Skaneateles, a very beautiful village, situated on a lake so-called. However, the proprietor of the coach seemed to have some private objection to this, and ordered the driver to go on in the contrary direction. We had to pocket the affront, and what was much more disagreeable, to travel an ugly, uninteresting road, instead of a picturesque one.

We had not proceeded many miles, when the vehicle broke down. We were not overturned or hurt, only tilted a little to one side. The driver, however, did not think it safe to proceed in this condition. The gentlemen got out, and searched the hedges and thickets for a piece of oak sufficiently strong and stout to repair, at least for a moment, the damage. At last they procured what they wanted, and having propped up the carriage after the best fashion they could, we proceeded at foot pace to the next village. While they were putting our conveyance into better order, Pierce Butler and I wandered away to a pretty water course, which, like all water in this country, was made to turn a mill. The coach being made sound once more, we packed ourselves into it, and progressed.

The sun set gloriously. Mr. Trelawney began talking about Greece, and getting a good deal excited. He presently burst forth into "The Isles of Greece", which he recited with amazing vehemence and earnestness. He reminded me of Kean several times—while he was declaiming he looked like tiger. 'This strange how, in spite of the contempt, even hatred, which he often expresses for England, and everything connected with it, his thoughts and plans and all the energies of his mind, seem ever bent upon changes to be wrought *in* England—freer government—purer laws—more equal rights.

Towards evening the heat became more and more oppressive, our coach was but ill cobbled, and leaned awfully to one side. I was so tired, so miserably sleepy, and so tortured with the side-ache from the cramped position in which I had been lying, that I just crawled into the first room of the inn where we alighted, and dropped down on the floor fast asleep. They roused me for supper, and soon after, I betook myself to bed. The heat was intolerable. I could not sleep—I never endured such suffocating heat.

Sunday, July 14th

ROSE at eight. After breakfast I wandered about the house in search of shade. I went into an empty room, opened the shutters, and got out upon a large colonnade which surrounded it. At about ten, our Exclusive Extra having driven to the door, we packed ourselves into it, and proceeded to Geneva, where we were to dine. The air was stifling and we were all gasping. Suddenly the lightning tore open the heavy clouds, the thunder rolled round the heavens, and the rain came down in torrents. We were away from all shelter and obliged to proceed through the storm. Our carpet bags, which were on the outside of the carriage, were soaked through, and we ourselves were soon in nearly as bad a plight. We arrived at about twelve o'clock at Cayuga, and we drew up at the inn door to await the end of the storm.

The storm having abated, we proceeded on our way, crossed a bridge a mile long over the Cayuga Lake, which was, however, still so veiled with scowling mist and clouds, that we could discern none of its features. At about three o'clock we reached Geneva, a small town situated on a lake called Seneca water. Here we dined. Pierce Butler had most providently brought silver forks with him, for the wretched two-pronged iron implements furnished by our host, were anything but clean or convenient.

After resting ourselves for a short time, we again took to our coach, and pursued our rote to Canandaigua, where we were to pass the night. The afternoon was bright and beautiful, and as the evening began to come on, we reached Canandaigua lake, a very beautiful sheet of water of considerable extent. We coasted for some time along its very margin. Leaving the water's edge, we proceeded about a quarter of a mile, and found ourselves at the door of an inn at Canandaigua, the principal among houses surrounding an open turfed space, like an English village green, across which ran the high road.

Supper was served to us in a large desolate-looking public room. After this, we came to the sitting room they had provided for us, a small comfortable apartment with a very finely toned piano in it. To this I forthwith sat down, and played and sang for a length of time. Late in the evening I left the instrument, and my father, Mr. Trelawney and I took a delightful stroll under the colonnade discussing Milton, many passages of which my father recited most beautifully, to my infinite delight. By and by they went in, and Pierce Butler came out to walk with me. We walked rapidly up and down, till the bleak blast became so keen that we were glad to take refuge in the house.

Monday, July 15th

OUR breakfast, which was extremely comfortable and clean, was served to us in our private room. It was

191

nine o'clock when we left Canandaigua, and as we were all a little done up with our previous two days, it was unanimously settled that we should proceed only to Rochester, distance of between thirty and forty miles, which we accomplished by two o'clock. Rochester, upon whose site, I understand, twenty years ago there stood hardly a house, is now a large and prosperous manufacturing town. The progress of life in this country is amazing.

The inn at which we alighted was large and comfortable. By the time we had seen our bedrooms and ordered dinner, we found we should have leisure before it was ready, to walk to the falls of the Genesee, the river on which Rochester stands, and which have some celebrity for their beauty. We walked up the main street and from this, turning off, we followed a wider road, and reached after half a mile's walk, a meadow skirted by a deep ravine, from whence we looked upon the falls. They were, I doubt not, once beautiful. But alas! the waters have been turned off to turn mills, and a thin curtain which falls over the rocks like a vapoury sheet of blue smoke, is all that remains of the Genesee falls. From a thousand dingy-looking mills and manufactories the poor little rivulets of labouring water come rushing through narrow dirty channels, all stained and foaming, and hot from their work, to throw themselves into the thin bosom of their parent stream. Truly, mills and steam-engines are wonderful things, and I know that men must live, but I wish it were not expedient to destroy what God has made so very beautiful, in order to make it useful.

We waited here for the passing of a train of rail-road carriages, which run between Rochester and a small village about three miles distant, where the river was said to be very beautiful. We hailed them as they went by and proceeded in them to their destination.

Then we walked along the high margin of the glen, looking down upon the deep bed of the river, enjoying the delicious fresh breeze. Nearing the town, we had to leave the brink of the river, and follow the dusty track of the railroad. When we reached Rochester, we dined. After which I went and lay down and slept till tea-time. When I came down to tea, I found the gentlemen profoundly busied; Pierce Butler writing home; Mr. Trelawney journalising; my father pouring over maps and road-books, to find if we could possibly get as far as Niagara tomorrow.

Tuesday, July 16th

HAD to get up before I'd half done my sleep. At six started from Rochester for Murray, where we purposed breakfasting. Just as we were nearing the inn at this place, and were all earnestly engaged in discussion, I suddenly felt a tremendous sort of stunning blow and as soon as I opened my eyes, found that the coach was overturned, lying completely on its side. I was curled up under my father, who by heaven's mercy did not suffocate me. Opposite sat Dall, white as a ghost, with her forehead cut open, and an awful stream of blood falling from it; by her stood Mr. Trelawney, also as pale as ashes; Pierce Butler was perched like a bird above us all on the edge of the doorway, which was open. The first thing I did was to cry as loud as ever I could, "I'm not hurt! I'm not hurt!" The next thing was to get my father up, in accomplishing which he trampled upon me most cruelly. As soon as I was relieved from his mountainous pressure, I got up, and saw two men carrying Mr. Trelawney into the house. I ran after as quickly as I could, and soon the house was like a hospital. They carried him into an upper room, and laid him on a bed, and here too, they brought Dall, all white and bleeding. I, with my clothes all torn and one shoulder cut and bruised, went from one to the other in utter dismay.

Soon, to my great relief, Mr. Trelawney revived, got up, and in the most skilful manner, plastered up poor Dall's brow. Pierce Butler went in search of my father, who had received a violent blow on his leg, and was halting about, looking after the baggage.

While the coach was being repaired, and the horses changed, we, bound up, bruised and aching, but still very merry, sat down to breakfast. Mr. Trelawney, who had been merely stunned, seized on the milk and honey and stuffed away with great zeal. Poor Dall was the most deplorable of the party, with a bloody handkerchief bound over one half of her face. I only ached a little, and Pierce Butler escaped with a scratch on his finger, so seeing that it was no worse, we thanked God and devoured.

Our route lay over what is called the Ridge road, a very remarkable tract, pursuing a high embankment, which was once the boundary of Lake Ontario. Our road, after leaving the Ridge road, was horrible. For some time before we reached Lockport, we were dragged over what is called a "corduroy" road, which consists merely of logs of wood laid close to each other—the natural inequalities of which produce a species of jolting superior to any other I ever felt, and administered little comfort, either to our bruised bones or apprehensive nerves.

We reached Lockport at about four o'clock. The house where we stopped appeared to be hardly finished. We ordered dinner, and I forthwith began kindling a fire, which was very welcome to us all. I was very much bruised with our morning's overturn, and went and lay down in my bedroom, where I slept profoundly.

A T nine o'clock we started from Lockport, and reached Lewistown about noon, and anxious inquiries were instituted as to how our luggage was to be forwarded when on the other side. A ferry boat and a ferry, however, were there, and thither we made our way. The ferry boat being at length procured, we got into it. The day was sultry; the heat intolerable. The water of the river Niagara is of a most peculiar colour, like a turquoise when it turns green.

Arrived on the other side, i.e. Canada, there was a second pause, as to how we were to get conveyed to the Falls. My father, Mr. Trelawney and Dall betook themselves to an inn by the roadside, which promised information and assistance. Pierce Butler and I clambered up the heights of Queenston, whence we looked towards Lake Ontario. He told me the history of the place; how his countrymen had thumped my countrymen upon this spot, and how the English general Brock had fallen near where we sat.

An uneasy-looking, rickety cart, without springs, was the sole conveyance we could obtain, and into this we packed ourselves. As we squeaked and creaked (I mean our vehicle) up the hill, I thought either my father's or Mr. Trelawney's weight, quite enough to have broken the whole thing down, but it did not happen. My mind was eagerly dwelling on what we were going to see, that sight which Trelawney said was the only one in the world which had not disappointed him. I felt absolutely nervous with expectation. The sound of the cataract is, they say, heard within fifteen miles when the wind sets favourably. Today however, there was no wind; the whole air was breathless with the heat of midsummer, and though we stopped the wagon once or twice to listen as we approached, all was the profoundest silence. When we were within about three miles of the Falls, we heard distinctly, though far off, the voice of the mighty cataract.

Looking over the woods which appeared to overhang the course of the river, we beheld one silver cloud rising slowly into the sky—the everlasting incense of the waters. A perfect frenzy of impatience seized upon me. I could have set off and run the whole way, and when at length the carriage stopped at the door of the Niagara House, waiting neither for my father, Dall nor Pierce Butler, I rushed through the hall and the garden, down the steep footpath cut in the rocks. I heard steps behind me, Trelawney was following me. Down, down I sprang, and along the narrow foot-path, divided only by a thicket from the tumultuous rapids, I saw through the boughs the white glimmer of that sea of foam. "Go on! go on! dont stop!", shouted Trelawney, and in another minute the thicket was passed. I stood upon Table Rock. Trelawney seized me by the arm, and without speaking a word, dragged me to the edge of the rapids, to the brink of the abyss. I saw Niagara—Oh God! who can describe that sight!!!

THE END

CHRONOLOGY

Summary of the Life of Frances Anne Kemble, 1809–1893 — Always Known as "Fanny"

November 27, 1809   Born in London. Her father, Charles Kemble, one of twelve children of Roger Kemble, strolling player. Her mother, Maria De Camp, French–Swiss, a dancer before her marriage.

1816–1818   Sent to school in Boulogne, but behaved badly and was brought home.

1818–1825   To Mme. Faudier's select establishment in Paris, where Fanny worked hard, and did well in French, Italian, music, and dancing.

1827   First meeting with Harriet St. Leger, an Anglo-Irish lady with whom Fanny corresponded regularly for many years.

1829   Charles Kemble in great financial difficulties. Theatre Royal, Covent Garden, of which he was part proprietor, losing money.

October 5, 1829   In order to retrieve the family fortunes, Fanny made a triumphant debut as Juliet at Covent Garden.

1829–1832   Fanny made very successful appearances in a variety of roles in London and in the provinces.

1832   Charles Kemble in financial trouble again. Sold his shares in Covent Garden.

August 1, 1932   Charles, Fanny, and her aunt Dall sailed for America.

September 1832–June 1834   The Kembles' tour of the principal cities of the eastern United States a great success. Fanny kept a detailed journal during the tour.

October 8, 1832   Fanny met Pierce Butler in Philadelphia. He was the wealthy heir to slave plantations in Georgia. He fell in love with Fanny, and followed her around on the tour.

June 7, 1834   Fanny and Pierce Butler married in Philadelphia. Charles Kemble returned to England alone.

1835   Fanny's *Journal*, kept during the tour, published in Philadelphia, against great opposition from her husband.

May 1835   Daughter Sarah born.

May 1838   Daughter Frances born.

During these years Fanny's independent spirit was at odds with her husband's ideas of wifely duty. Many clashes of personality.

1838–1839   Differences between Fanny and her husband came to a head after a stay on his slave plantations. She recorded her horror of slavery in *Journal of a Residence on a Georgian Plantation*, published in London in 1863.

1845   After several attempts at reconciliation, Fanny left her husband and two little girls and returned to England.

1846–1847   Fanny spent a year in Italy with her sister, Adelaide Sartoris, a former opera singer. *Year of Consolation* was published in 1947.

1847   Back in England, Fanny tried to resume her stage career, with little success.

1849   Pierce Butler divorced Fanny for desertion and obtained custody of the two children.

1850   Fanny embarked on a very successful second career, giving readings of Shakespeare in London, the provinces, and America. She made enough money in the next twenty years to buy a house in Lenox, New England.

1876   Harriet St. Leger, now a very old lady, returned to Fanny all the letters she had received from her over the years.

1878   Using these letters and her own recollections (not always very accurate) Fanny published three volumes of *Records of a Girlhood*, from her childhood to her marriage in 1834. This work was a great success.

1882   *Records of a Later Life* dealing with her life from 1834 to 1838, is very reticent about her marriage. It was published in three volumes.

1884   Two volumes of *Further Records* published—rather disorganised and many sections undated; it ends in 1877.

The last years of her life Fanny spent happily with friends or with her daughters in America, London, Leamington Spa, and Strat-ford-on-Avon.

1889 *Far Away and Long Ago* was published in New York.
1893 Fanny died in London.

NOTES

Colonel Sibell: a New York business man, a militia colonel.

Mr. William Hodgkinson: an Englishman, settled for many years in Boston. He and his sister, Harriet, were the most congenial to me of all our fellow passengers. He was, I think, very fond of me, and showed his regard by endeavouring to make my aunt and my father aware of Mr. Butler's character when first that gentleman paid his addresses to me. But I was "in love", and paid little heed to his cautions, which reached me second hand through my aunt.

Miss Harriet Hodgkinson: a young English girl, going to Boston with her brother.

Captain Whaite: captain of the *Pacific.*

Mr. James Bell: Englishman established for many years in New York, where he made a fortune.

Harriet St. Leger: an Irish spinster lady, living near Dublin. For many years she and Fanny maintained a regular correspondence. Harriet's letters to Fanny do not survive, but before she died, Harriet returned to Fanny all *her* letters. Fanny used these letters as the basis for her autobiographies *Record of a Girlhood* and *Further Records.*

Thomas Moore: an Irishman, the composer of the words and music of many popular ballads, e.g. "The Last Rose of Summer, "The Minstrel Boy" and many others. Fanny met him in Edinburgh when staying there with her cousin in 1828, and sang duets with him.

Mr. Staley: a young Yorkshireman, engaged for many years in business in Philadelphia.

Mr. Curtis: first mate of the *Pacific.*

Mr. Wallack: a leading American actor.

Mr. Philip Hone: a wealthy New York auctioneer and former mayor of the city. He and his brother Isaac, and his nephew, Henry, were very attentive and civil to us on our first visit to New York.

Vincent Decamp: lessee of the Theatre Royal, Montreal, and my mother's brother.

Ogden Hoffman: a very charming and intelligent person, an eminent member of the New York bar.

'Dall', Adelaide Decamp: my mother's second sister. She had been disappointed in love as a young girl, and had devoted her life to caring for my mother's family. She accompanied me on my American tour, and died in Boston in 1834 as the result of a carriage accident.

Mr. Bancroft: an Englishman, chargé d'affaires in New York.

Captain Martin: a Captain in the British army.

Mr. Henry Berkley: one of the illegitimate children of the Earl of Berkley. He was one of the most impertinent and profligate men I have ever known. He was an intimate friend of Mr. Pierce Butler, and it is to this Englishman's example and precept that I attribute much of Mr. Butler's subsequent profligacy and want of principle.

Essex: a negro servant from the *Pacific.*

Mr. Keppel: incompetent actor, with whom I had to play.

Isaac Hone: brother of Mr. Philip Hone.

Mr. Gaston: a gentleman from Georgia, introduced to me by Mr. Hone.

Charles Kean: actor, son of the celebrated Edmund Kean.

Kean: Edmund Kean, famous for his Richard the 3rd, and Iago, at Covent Garden and Drury Lane.

Mr. Pierce Butler: a wealthy young man from Philadelphia. The owner of slave plantations in Georgia. He was strongly attracted to me at our first meeting, and frequently sent me flowers, played the flute in the theater orchestras so as to be near me, and accompanied me and my father on the latter part of their tour. We were married at Christ Church, Philadelphia, on June 7, 1834.

Mrs. Davenport: the English actress who played the Nurse in the production of *Romeo and Juliet* at Covent Garden, in which I made my stage debut on October 5, 1829.

Mr. Nicholas Biddle: president of the U.S. Bank, and his son *Edward Biddle*.

Mrs. Dulaney: wife of Colonel Dulaney of Alexandria, Virginia. One of the most beautiful and charming women I had ever known.

Der Freischutz very popplar opera by Weber, produced at Covent Garden in 1824–25. I conceived a teenage passion for the composer.

Lord Mulgrave: governor of Jamaica, and keen on amateur theatricals. A good friend of Charles Kemble.

Lord and Lady Ellesmere: formerly Sir Francis and Lady Egerton, whom I first met when I was staying near their house, Oatlands Park, Weybridge, Surrey, with my mother.

Emily Chapman: daughter of an eminent physician of Philadelphia. Had been courted by Pierce Butler before he met me, and who describes his dealings with the lady as "the most cruel and dishonourable of which a man can be guilty towards a woman."

Sully: an well-known American portrait painter, who painted an excellent likeness of myself and of my father.

Dr. Channing: a Unitarian minister, strongly anti-salvery. It was he who introduced me to the movements for emancipation of slaves.

John Edward Trelawney: friend of Byron and Shelley, and author of *Adventures of a Younger Son*, and *Recollections of Byron and Shelley*.

Catherine Sedgwick: an important literary figure in New England. She and her family became my closest friends in America.

BIBLIOGRAPHY

Books by Fanny Kemble

Journal. Philadelphia: Carey, Lea & Blanchard, 1835.
Year of Consolation. London: Moxon, 1847.
Journal of a Residence on a Georgian Plantation, 1838–39. New
    York: Harper, 1863; edited with an introduction by John A.
    Scott. Athens: University of Georgia Press, 1984.
Records of a Girlhood. London: Bentley, 1878.
Records of a Later Life. London: Bentley, 1882.
Further Records. London: Bentley, 1884.
Far Away and Long Ago. New York: 1889.

Books About Fanny Kemble

Armstrong, Margaret. *Fanny Kemble.* New York: Macmillan, 1938.
Bobbé, Dorothie. *Fanny Kemble.* New York, 1938.
Driver, Leota. *Fanny Kemble.* Chapel Hill: University of North
    Carolina Press, 1933.
Fitzgerald, Edward. *Letters to Fanny Kemble.* London: Macmillan,
    1902.
Furnas, J. C. *Fanny Kemble, Leading Lady of the 19th Century Stage.*
    New York: Dial Press, 1982.
Gibbs, Henry. *Yours Affectionately, Fanny.* London: Jarrolds, 1945.
Marshall, Dorothy. *Fanny Kemble.* London: Weidenfeld &
    Nicolson, 1977.

Ransome, Eleanor, ed. *The Terrific Kemble*. London: Hamish
Hamilton, 1978.
Rushmore, Robert. *Fanny Kemble*. New York, 1970.
Wright, Constance. *Fanny Kemble and the Lovely Land*. London:
Robert Hale, 1972.

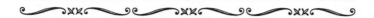

INDEX

DATE DUE

GAYLORD			PRINTED IN U.S.A.